The American Year

David Fermer

The American Year

Teacher's notes and activities
Ruth Steffens

Ernst Klett Sprachen
Stuttgart

1. Auflage   1 ⁶ ⁵ ⁴ ³ ² | 2018 17 16 15 14

Redaktion: Debby Böhm, Don Haupt
Layoutkonzeption: Elmar Feuerbach
Illustrationen: Matthias Pflügner
Gestaltung und Satz: DOPPELPUNKT, Stuttgart / Swabianmedia Stuttgart
Umschlaggestaltung: Elmar Feuerbach
Titelbild: Shutterstock (Stephen Coburn), New York
Foto Seite 45: iStockphoto (BDphoto), Calgary, Alberta
Druck und Bindung: Digitaldruck Tebben, Biessenhofen
Printed in Germany

978-3-12-577343-1

Inhaltsverzeichnis

Synopses

1. Will you be my Valentine?

16-year-old Mitch, who suffers from Down Syndrome, has designed a beautiful Valentine's game to win the heart of the high school beauty, Claire. But is Mitch really the boy Claire is looking for?

Themen: Valentine's Day: February 14th
            Schools in the USA

2. Forgiving Katrina

As the first Mardi Gras parade takes place in a devastated New Orleans, Sadie sees her home town through new eyes and reflects on the events leading up to Hurricane Katrina.

Themen: Mardi Gras: Epiphany
            Hurricane Katrina

3. Opa Joe

It's the first Passover that Lucy's family will be celebrating since the death of Lucy's grandfather, Opa Joe. As 16-year-old Lucy prepares the Seder meal, she reflects on the journey her grandfather once made from the concentration camps of Europe to New York.

Themen: Passover: March/April
            Germans in the USA: The story of immigration

4. ABC

From being just another American-born Chinese boy in San Francisco, James feels completely out of place when his family moves to a small town in Wyoming. To make matters worse, his first day at his new high school is April 1st and the school bully is out to play a prank on him.

Themen: April Fool's Day: April 1st
            Asian communities in the USA

5. Escape to the USA

On the night of Cinco de Mayo, when Hispanics across America celebrate their cultural roots, hundreds of illegal immigrants make their way towards the U.S.-Mexican border in search of a better future, amongst them a father and son who both know that their chances of making it are slim.

Themen: Cinco de Mayo: May 5th
            Secret lives: Illegal immigration in the USA

6. Divided Country

Two young boys play out the American Civil War in the woods around their home town of Fulton, Kentucky. But when they stumble across an unmarked grave, their game turns into a conflict of their own.

Themen: Memorial Day: Last Monday in May
            Brother against brother: The American Civil War

7. Freedom

19-year-old "Scoop" can't help seeing the irony of being released from his first-ever prison term on July 4th, but is the young man from Philadelphia really ready for his independence?

Themen: Independence Day: July 4th
           Locked up: The U.S. prison system

8. Patriot

September 11 is a day of national mourning in the USA. For the Hispanic teenager Carmen it's also a day to remember her father, a cleaner who was killed in the Twin Towers. While everyone praises her father as a patriot, his diaries tell a different story.

Themen: Patriot Day: September 11th
           The Hispanic community in the USA

9. Indian Elvis

Looking back from his death bed, Sherman Klah, a member of the Native American tribe of the Navaho Nation, recalls his first performance at his reservation's Pow-wow, an annual Native American celebration, when he sang as the "Indian Elvis".

Themen: Native American Day: Fourth Friday in September
           The destruction of Native American culture in the USA

10. 13th Street

When a group of kids go trick and treating on October 31 in Detroit, their parents make it very clear to their children where they can – and cannot – go. An evening of fun turns into a night of horror as a group of teenagers dare to go into 13th Street.

Themen: Halloween: October 31st
           Detroit: The decline of an American city

11. Servant of God

As America takes to the road to join their families for Thanksgiving, an Evangelical pastor is running late. His family's concerns are justified when the police turn up on their doorstep and start asking awkward questions about the man who calls himself the "Servant of God".

Themen: Thanksgiving: Fourth Thursday in November
           Hallelujah: Mega-Churches in the USA

12. African Roots

1972. A white mother brings her black son to see the African-American celebration of Kwanzaa in Hawaii.
When the 11-year-old boy tells a guest about his dreams of becoming the first black President of America, his aspirations are met by laughter. The boy's name is Barack Obama.

Themen: Kwanzaa: December 26th
           Barack Obama: The first black President

Vorwort

Diese Sammlung englischsprachiger Kurzgeschichten bietet ideales Lesematerial für den anspruchsvollen Englischunterricht ab der 8. Klasse. Die Geschichten sind jugendnah und zeitgemäß. Sie behandeln ein breites Spektrum aktueller Themen, z. B. illegale Einwanderung oder das amerikanische Strafsystem sowie historische Begebenheiten wie den amerikanischen Bürgerkrieg oder die Bürgerrechtsbewegung der 60er Jahre.

Die Geschichten werden jeweils vor dem Hintergrund eines amerikanischen Feiertags, bzw. einem in den USA gefeierten Festes, erzählt und bieten damit einen weiteren Lernaspekt. Von Valentine's Day bis zu Halloween, von Passover zum wenig bekannten afro-amerikanischen Erntefest Kwanzaa, folgen die Geschichten einem kalendarischen Ablauf. Sie müssen aber keineswegs in dieser Reihenfolge gelesen werden. Die *mini stories* sind im Englischunterricht flexibel einsetzbar.

Ein Infoblatt und drei Seiten mit Lehrermaterialien begleiten jede Geschichte. Das Infoblatt bietet kurzweilige Hintergrundinformation zu den jeweiligen Feier-/Festtagen und zum Inhalt der Geschichte. Sowohl die Infoblätter als auch die Geschichten sind mit einer englisch-deutschen Vokabelliste ausgestattet, um das Lesen der Texte zu erleichtern.

Ich wünsche Ihnen und Ihren Schülern viel Lesefreude! Enjoy!

David Fermer

Hinweise zu den Teacher's Notes

Die vorliegenden Unterrichtsvorschläge sind so konzipiert, dass die Beschäftigung mit der Geschichte selbst in einer Doppelstunde geschehen kann. Innerhalb dieser Doppelstunde wird die Geschichte in drei Phasen rezipiert, die sich in der ersten Kopiervorlage wiederspiegeln:

Pre-reading activities: Sie dienen der Vorentlastung, z. B. des Vokabulars oder des Verständnisses, und wecken Erwartungen (durchaus auch falsche!) und Neugier auf die Geschichte.

While-reading activities: Die Geschichten werden meist gehört und dabei gelesen; im Einzelfall kann ein anderes Vorgehen sinnvoll sein. Während des Hörens/Lesens bzw. unmittelbar im Anschluss daran werden die vorher erläuterten *while-reading activities* ausgeführt. Sie dienen oft der Sicherung des Erstverständnisses.

Post-reading activities: Die weiterführenden Aufgaben sollen zu einer tiefergehenden Beschäftigung mit der Geschichte anregen.

Die zweite Kopiervorlage dient dann der Erweiterung bzw. Differenzierung. Sie beschäftigt sich nicht mehr nur unmittelbar mit der Handlung, sondern auch mit Hintergründen, die sich auch auf den in der Geschichte angesprochenen Feiertag/ Festtag beziehen.

Die *Teacher's Notes* enthalten Durchführungsvorschläge und Anregungen für Differenzierungen, Erweiterungen, Hausaufgaben. Lösungen und Erwartungshorizonte für die Arbeitsaufträge finden Sie am Ende dieses Heftes.

Will you be my Valentine? by David Fermer

Mitch was very excited about his plan. He'd worked everything out in detail: the timing, the clues, the idea with the throne (a reference to Claire's performance as Juliet in the school play), the start and finish. He called it his "Valentine Trail". He'd set it all up the day before, after school, and timed it to exactly 15 minutes.

5 Claire would probably need a bit longer, but she would still be able to complete it during the morning break. Mitch couldn't wait to see her face when she got to the end.

Mitch was so excited on the morning of Valentine's Day that he could hardly breathe. The boys and girls came crashing into the classroom after the morning

10 bell, talking, shouting, laughing. They were so loud. Even louder than usual. Mitch didn't understand why they always laughed so much. Watching and listening was far more interesting. Mitch was an expert at that. He'd been watching and listening all his life.

When he saw Claire come into the classroom that morning, the morning of

15 February 14th, he thought she looked particularly beautiful. It was as if she'd made a special effort just for him. He couldn't wait for his "Valentine Trail" to begin.

There was more laughter and giggling that morning as the boys circled around the pretty girls, joking about Valentine's Day, flirting. Lance even asked Eve if she would be his Valentine, but he was only playing with her. Eve went red in the face,

20 and Lance laughed and laughed, slapping his friends on the back as they shared the joke with him. Mitch thought they were a bunch of clowns. But they were in school, not the circus.

Josh was there, too. Juliet's Romeo. Mitch saw Claire look at him as he came into the classroom, saw the flush of color redden her cheeks before she looked

25 away. Mitch hoped that he didn't turn red when he looked at Claire, but Claire seldom looked at him anyway.

The first few lessons were as dull as watching paint dry. Something about equations. Mitch was terrible at Math. He just couldn't get his head around it. Numbers were fine as long as they followed each other in the correct order – 1, 2,

30 3, 4, 5, etc. – but as soon as the order changed, as soon as Mr. Alvarez told them to do things with numbers that didn't follow that order, Mitch didn't know what to do. He would sit at his desk and look out the window until the lesson was over.

When the bell rang for first break, Mitch felt his heart miss a beat. This was it. The start of the trail. He watched Claire put her books into her bag and followed

35 her out of the room, keeping his distance. She went straight to her locker, as he knew she would, where the first clue was waiting: a red heart with the words:

"Be my Valentine, take my heart,
it lies near water, beneath great art."

Mitch saw Claire take down the note and read it. She looked around to see if

40 anyone was watching her. Josh walked past and smiled.

1 **work sth out** *etw. aus-arbeiten*
2 **clue** *Hinweis*
2 **reference** *Anspielung*
2 **performance** *Auftritt*
3 **trail** *Weg*
10 **bell** *Läuten*
10 **usual** *üblich*
15 **particularly** *besonders*
16 **effort** *Mühe*
17 **to giggle** *kichern*
20 **to slap sb** *jdm einen Klaps geben*
21 **bunch** *Haufen*
24 **to flush** *erröten*
27 **dull** *langweilig*
27 **to dry** *trocknen*
28 **equation** *Gleichung*
29 **order** *Reihenfolge*
35 **to keep one's distance** *Abstand halten*
35 **locker** *Schließfach*
38 **beneath** *unter*

"Hi, Claire! What's up?" he said, but he didn't stop for an answer.

Claire read the message again, then followed Josh out to the yard. Mitch knew she was smart, but she was faster than he thought. She went straight to the school mosaic by the fountain and found the second clue:

45
"I love your smile, I love the way you dress.
Come to the basement and be my princess."

Claire looked around again, but she didn't see Mitch, who was watching her from the main entrance. She put the note in her bag, hurried to the side door and slipped inside. Mitch went into the main building and ran down the stairs, taking
50 two steps at a time, just as he'd done the day before. He knew he'd get there before her, even though it wasn't easy for him to run so fast. He almost fell over a couple of times.

He was down in the basement in no time. He opened the door, took out a flashlight and went over to the throne in the middle of the room. He had just sat
55 down and put the plastic crown on his head when he heard footsteps outside. He turned off his flashlight and waited.

The door opened. Light fell onto the floor. Mitch saw Claire's silhouette in the stairwell.

"Josh?" she said as she stepped into the room. "Is that you?"
60 Mitch heard the excitement in her voice, heard her fingers searching for the light switch on the wall. But when the lights went on, the look on her face wasn't the one Mitch was expecting. She didn't break into a smile and run across the room and throw herself into his arms, thanking him for the beautiful surprise and telling him, *yes, she wanted to be his princess*. Her jaw simply dropped. She
65 frowned.

"Mitch?" she said. She came up to him slowly, her eyes searching his face, taking in the crown on his head, the throne beneath him. "Mitch ..." she said again. "What are you doing?"

"Will you be my Valentine?" Mitch asked boldly, and – after a moment of
70 uncertainty – a smile appeared on Claire's face for the first time. A sad smile.

"Oh, Mitch!" she said. "I can't ..."

Mitch knew why.

He turned away to hide his tears. The crown fell off his head and rolled across the floor. It came to a halt at a broken mirror leaning against the wall. Mitch
75 looked at his own reflection in the dirty glass. It was because he was different. He felt normal, but he knew that people didn't see him that way. He had Down Syndrome, that was all. Apart from that, he was just like anybody else.

"Maybe next year, yeah?" said Claire, and she bent down and kissed him gently on the cheek. "Thanks for the surprise, Mitch. It was great."

* * *

43 **smart** *schlau*
46 **basement** *Keller*
49 **to slip inside** *hinein-schleichen*
54 **flashlight** *Taschenlampe*
55 **crown** *Krone*
55 **footsteps** *Schritte*
58 **stairwell** *Treppenhaus*
60 **excitement** *Aufregung*
61 **light switch** *Lichtschalter*
64 **jaw** *Kiefer*
65 **to frown** *die Stirn runzeln*
67 **to take in** *erfassen*
69 **boldly** *mutig*
70 **uncertainty** *Zweifel*
70 **to appear** *erscheinen*
73 **to hide** *verstecken*
74 **mirror** *Spiegel*
75 **reflection** *Spiegelbild*
78 **to bend down** *sich bücken*
78 **gently** *sanft*

Valentine's Day: February 14th

Valentine's Day takes place every year on February 14th and is also known as "The Feast of Saint Valentine". There are various theories about the origins of Valentine's Day, but the most popular one goes back to a priest called Valentine who lived in the 3rd century in Italy. The Roman Emperor at the time, Claudius II,
5 thought that unmarried men made better soldiers, but Valentine helped soldiers who were in love by performing weddings for them, although it was forbidden. Claudius put Saint Valentine into prison. It is said that while in prison, Saint Valentine healed the blind daughter of his jailer before being executed on February 14. After his death, the jailer's family converted to Christianity and
10 Valentine became a saint. But it wasn't until 1537 that England's King Henry VII declared February 14th the holiday of St. Valentine's Day and started a tradition which continues today. Traditionally, Valentine's Day involves the sending of cards or flowers or other small gifts by secret admirers. More than 110 million red roses are sold every year on Valentine's Day in the United States alone, and over 145
15 million Valentine's cards are sent. Statistics show that generally men buy flowers and women choose to send cards. In the USA, teachers receive more Valentine's Day cards than anybody else.

1 **to take place** *stattfinden*
2 **various** *verschieden*
6 **forbidden** *verboten*
8 **to heal sb** *jdn heilen*
8 **jailer** *Gefängniswärter*
8 **to execute sb** *jdn hinrichten*
9 **to convert sb** *jdn bekehren*
11 **to declare** *verkünden*
13 **admirer** *Verehrer*
15 **generally** *normalerweise*

Schools in the USA

In the USA, all children have to attend school, but the age of children starting
20 and finishing school can be different from state to state. In some states, children begin school at the age of 5, in others as late as 7. In states like Oklahoma, Virginia and the District of Columbia, children have to attend school between the ages of 5 and 18. In others, such as Idaho and Minnesota, parents only have to send their children to school from the ages of 7 to 16. In general, elementary school goes
25 from grades 1 to 5, while secondary education is split into junior and senior high school. Middle school or junior high school goes from grades 6 to 8/9, while grades 9/10 to 12 are covered by senior high school. In senior high the different grades are also known by other names: grade 9 is called "Freshman", grade 10 is "Sophomore" year, grade 11 "Junior", and grade 12 "Senior". The same names are
30 used for the first four years in college or university. About 80 million children and teenagers attend school in the USA (that's almost the entire population of Germany!) and there are more than 7 million teachers. In the U.S., inclusion has been a part of school culture since the 1970s. Today three out of five students with learning disabilities attend their local school.

19 **to attend** *besuchen*
20 **different** *anders*
24 **elementary school** *Grundschule*
25 **secondary education** *Sekundarstufe*
34 **learning disability** *Lernbehinderung*

© Ernst Klett Sprachen GmbH, Stuttgart 2014 | www.klett.de | Alle Rechte vorbehalten
Kopieren für den eigenen Unterrichtsgebrauch gestattet.
ISBN 978-3-12-577343-X

Ziel: Vorentlastung; Reaktivierung vorhandenen Wortschatzes; Thema: Liebe

Aufgabe 1: Der Titel *Will you be my Valentine* muss vor dem Lesen der Geschichte geklärt werden, da nicht vorausgesetzt werden kann, dass jeder diesen Valentinskartengruß versteht.

Da der *Valentine's Day* so unmittelbar mit dem Thema „Liebe" verbunden ist, kann hier viel an bekanntem Wortschatz aktiviert werden. Die SuS fertigen dazu eine *mind map* auf A4-Papier an und verzieren ggf. die gefundenen Wörter mit Bildern, Symbolen etc. Für schwächere Lerngruppen können außer dem Wort *love* z. B. folgende Begriffe an der Tafel vorgegeben werden:

> *dating* (e.g. to go out), *symptoms* (e.g. to blush), *Romeo and Juliet* (e.g. teenagers), *symbols* (e.g. heart).

Ziele: Hörverstehen eines unbekannten Textes; Formulierung von Vorerwartungen

Die Geschichte wird in mehrere Abschnitte unterteilt und zunächst nur von CD vorgespielt.

An den entsprechenden Stellen (jeweils nach den kurzen „Reimen") wird das Abspielen der Geschichte unterbrochen und die SuS bearbeiten die Fragen und Aufgaben der Kopiervorlage.

Die SuS betrachten die bisherige Handlung und spekulieren mit den Vorerwartungen an eine Liebesgeschichte, wie die Geschichte weitergehen könnte. Dabei sollte sichergestellt werden, dass der Inhalt der kurzen Abschnitte verstanden wurde.

- Abschnitt 1: bis zum 1. Liebesgedicht (Zeile 1–38), anschließend Aufgabe 2a)
- Abschnitt 2: bis zum 2. Liebesgedicht (Zeile 39–46), anschließend Aufgabe 2b)
- Abschnitt 3: bis *A sad smile.* (Zeile 70), anschließend Aufgabe 2c)

Im Anschluss wird das Ende der Geschichte vorgespielt. Danach kann der Text ausgeteilt und noch einmal gelesen werden.

Ziel: Textsicherung; Textverständnis; kreatives Umgehen mit dem Text

Die SuS diskutieren, wie sie das Ende der Geschichte beurteilen (auch als schriftliche Hausaufgabe möglich):

> *Does the story have a happy or a sad ending? Why?*

Hieran schließen sich Aufgabe 3 und KV 1.2 als Möglichkeit zur Textsicherung bzw. zum kreativen Weiterarbeiten an.

Mögliche Differenzierung für stärkere Kurse:

> *Can you find hints in the text that Mitch is not like the other children?*

---

pre-reading
KV 1.1, Aufg. 1
ca. 10 min.

while-reading
KV 1.1, Aufg. 2
ca. 45–55 min.

post-reading

KV 1.1, Aufg. 3
KV 1.2
ca. 15–25 min.

13

1. Valentine

The title of the story you are about to read is "Will you be my Valentine?". You often find this sentence on Valentine's cards. What does it mean?

☐ I don't know your name but I'll call you Valentine.

☐ I love you. Do you want to go out with me?

☐ I think Valentine is a stupid name.

☐ I like you. How about a date on Valentine's Day?

2. Listening: Will you be my Valentine?

a) Listen to the story and answer the following questions after the first stop. Take notes.

Boys: *You are Mitch*
1) Would you want Claire to discover you at this point?
2) How would you feel at this point?
3) Is this a good idea or a stupid idea if you like a girl? Would you do this, too?

Girls: *You are Claire*
1) What would you think at this point?
2) How would you feel at this point?
3) What would you do at this point?

b) Listen to the story and answer the following questions after the second stop. Take notes.
4) Who does Claire probably think the cards are from? Why?
5) What do you expect she is going to do at this point?
6) If you got this card or a similar one, would you go to the basement? Why / why not?

c) Listen to the story and do the following tasks after the third stop. Take notes.
Step 1: Please finish the story in four to five sentences. You have got 10 minutes to do so.
Step 2: Get together in groups of four. Read out your story endings to the group, then choose the best (or cleverest, funniest, most surprising) ending.
Step 3: Read the best ending of each group to the class.

d) Now listen to the end of the story.

3. Choose one of the following tasks:

a) Draw Mitch's Valentine's trail in three pictures. Find a good caption[1] for each picture.

OR

b) Draw / write your own Valentine's card. Write your own love poem (two or four lines). Maybe you can say something nice about your "Valentine", or you could come up with a riddle, too. Make your card look lovely.

---

[1] **caption** *Bildunterschrift*

Valentine's Day

A teen magazine is doing a Valentine's Day Special. Find three more questions and answers for this quiz.

❤ Are you romantic? ❤

1. Your idea of a perfect Valentine's gift is:

   a) a teddy bear with a pink heart on it, saying "I love you"   (5)
   b) flowers   (3)
   c) a mountain bike   (1)

2. _____

   _____ (5)

   _____ (3)

   _____ (1)

3. _____

   _____ (5)

   _____ (3)

   _____ (1)

4. _____

   _____ (5)

   _____ (3)

   _____ (1)

Now exchange your quiz with somebody else's quiz and find out, whether YOU are romantic.

↓   ↓   ↓

16–20 points: ❤ ❤ ❤	**8–15 points: ❤ ❤**	**1–7 points: ❤**
Your name isn't *Romeo* by any chance? Or *Juliet*? You are very romantic. You love long walks in the moonlight and candlelight dinners with your sweetheart. But don't forget: nobody can live on cloud nine forever.	In everyday life you are a down-to-earth person, but when you are in love you can be quite romantic, too. You don't mind telling your boyfriend or girlfriend how much you love him or her.	You are not a very romantic person. A perfect time with your partner is probably a bike trip or an evening in front of the television. But don't forget: everybody likes to hear that he or she is loved or to get a little surprise present. Even you, right?

Forgiving Katrina by David Fermer

"We're going back tomorrow," said Sadie into the phone, but her words were met by silence. All she could hear was the sound of Maurice breathing on the other end of the line.

"What about you?" she asked. "When are you coming back?"

5 "I don't know."

Maurice sounded distant.

"You are coming back, aren't you?" she asked.

"Maybe."

Sadie found it difficult to forgive Maurice for that word. "Maybe." It wasn't the
10 answer she had been expecting. It wasn't the answer she wanted to hear. It had taken days for her to reach her boyfriend. He was staying with family in Florida. His cell phone wasn't working. She'd lost hers in the storm. But after speaking to him, she felt worse rather than better.

"Maybe." It almost sounded like an apology.

15 Maurice had left New Orleans two days before Hurricane Katrina. Sadie and her family had stayed. But as the storm raged over the city and the levees broke, flooding the streets, Sadie and her family had no other choice but to leave. The city was in ruins. There was no running water, no electricity. Drinking water and food were contaminated. It was as if the storm had sucked New Orleans in,
20 chewed on it and spit it out. The National Guard had come and rescued people and started an evacuation. Sadie's family was put on a bus and sent to Texas. Now her father couldn't wait to get back home. And Sadie couldn't wait, either.

Returning was easier said than done. Sadie and her family arrived home to find their house smelling of rot. The water, which had come up to the ceiling, was
25 now gone, but the damage could be seen everywhere. The wooden floor was black with mud. Mold was eating away at the wallpaper. The colors had washed out of the family photographs hanging in the living room. Outside, the street was a river of rubble. It was as if someone had tipped a gigantic bucket of mud over their neighborhood.

30 It took them months to clean up. First they cleared out the house, Sadie, her dad and two brothers, working all day, every day, until their fingers were bloody and their knees were red and sore. *We are stronger than this storm*, they told themselves. *Nothing can break us.*

With no school to attend, Sadie threw herself into the task of cleaning up
35 everything. The pile of rubble outside their house grew steadily. During the day they left their windows open so the sun could dry the walls. They used knives to scratch away the dried mud between the floorboards.

And while she cleared and cleaned and hauled and repainted, she couldn't help thinking about Maurice in Florida. Sadie had called him again after coming
40 back to New Orleans, but they had nothing more to say to each other. "Maybe"

2 **silence** *Stille*
2 **to breathe** *atmen*
6 **distant** *abwesend*
10 **to expect** *erwarten*
11 **to reach** *erreichen*
12 **cell phone** *Handy*
14 **apology** *Entschuldigung*
16 **to rage** *toben*
16 **levee** *Damm*
17 **to flood** *überschwemmen*
19 **contaminated** *ver-schmutzt*
19 **to suck in** *hier: aufsaugen*
20 **to chew** *kauen*
24 **rot** *Verfall*
24 **ceiling** *Decke*
25 **damage** *Schaden*
26 **mud** *Schlamm*
26 **mold** *Schimmel*
26 **wallpaper** *Tapete*
28 **rubble** *Trümmer*
28 **bucket** *Eimer*
32 **sore** *wund*
35 **steadily** *stetig*
37 **to scratch** *kratzen*
38 **to haul** *schleppen*

was the only word that stayed in Sadie's head, and she still couldn't forgive him for saying it. The two of them had been dating for almost a year before the storm. Maurice had told her he loved her. She'd almost said it back, but each time she'd stopped herself. *Not now. Not yet. It's still too early.* So she hadn't told him she
45 loved him, even though she did, and now, back in New Orleans, she felt betrayed.

So when the first people began to talk about Mardi Gras, the annual festival which was at the heart of New Orleans' cultural identity, and whether the city could afford to celebrate it after Katrina or not, Sadie was quick to voice her opinion. "Of course, we have to celebrate! Now more than ever. If we don't
50 celebrate Mardi Gras, this city is dead."

Sadie had celebrated Mardi Gras ever since she could remember. Her father was a member of one of the city's oldest *krewes*. Every year she helped him make his costume, painted the *krewe's* parade float with him, marched along the streets of the city day after day, singing and dancing. She loved the music, loved the
55 craziness of it all, the mix of cultures: southern and Caribbean, French and Spanish, Native American and Creole, jazz, big band, Cajun. Mardis Gras was a celebration of life, a celebration of the city of New Orleans.

Others from the neighborhood shared Sadie's opinion, and those who had come back to the city soon began to make preparations for Mardi Gras. They took
60 their floats out of the garage and let them dry in the sun. They cut away the rotten wood, cleaned off the mold and repainted them. Some even created new designs which criticized the government's handling of the emergency. Too little, too late. Black America left to rot. At night, they sat together and made new costumes from old clothes. The *krewes* talked to the town hall and got a permit to
65 parade down Saint Charles Avenue to Canal Street. Skeptics all around the country looked on and said it would never happen. How could a city which had been brought to its knees by Hurricane Katrina stand up and party?

But it did. Only four months after the terrible storm, Mardi Gras took place.

That year, in February 2006, the skeptics were silenced as a small parade
70 danced and sang its way down the streets of the French Quarter. The trumpets were clean and shiny, the trombones spotless, the drums loud and dazzling. And, as she danced and sang with them, Sadie felt all the bad things in her life fall away. All the pain and sadness of the last few months disappeared. Suddenly everything made sense. And when she saw Maurice in the crowd, a familiar face
75 she thought she'd never see again, she ran up to him and kissed him and took his hand in hers. And as they stood there together and looked at the scenes of color and music around them, Sadie finally spoke the three words she had been meaning to say for a long time: "I forgive you."

* * *

42 to date sb *mit jdm ausgehen*
45 betrayed *betrogen*
46 annual *jährlich*
48 to afford *sich leisten*
48 to voice *aussprechen*
52 krewe *Karnevalsgruppe*
53 float *Karnevalswagen*
61 rotten *verfault*
62 handling *Handhabung*
64 permit *Genehmigung*
65 skeptic *Zweifler*
68 to take place *stattfinden*
69 to silence *zum Schweigen bringen*
71 trombone *Posaune*
71 spotless *makellos*
71 dazzling *überwältigend*
74 to make sense *einen Sinn ergeben*
74 familiar *vertraut*

Mardi Gras: Epiphany

Mardi Gras is a festival which takes place in New Orleans, Louisiana, every year, usually in February. Mardi Gras is similar to carnival *(Fasching)* in the rest of the Roman Catholic world. It is a period of street parades and parties with music, dancing, singing and colorful costumes. Officially Mardi Gras begins on Epiphany
5 *(Dreikönigsfest)* and ends on Ash Wednesday *(Aschermittwoch)*, but, like carnival in Cologne or Rio de Janiero, it is mainly the last week of festivities which is important. Mardi Gras was brought to the USA by French colonists at the end of the 17th century. Large parts of what is today Louisiana used to belong to France. The French colonies in North America stretched from New Orleans on the Gulf of
10 Mexico to Montreal in Canada. It was only in 1763 that the French lost their North American colonies to the British and Spanish. The name Mardi Gras means "Fat Tuesday" in French and refers to the day of feasting before the start of Lent *(Fastenzeit)* on Ash Wednesday when traditional Christians fast. The street parades in New Orleans are organized by carnival groups called "krewes". The
15 krewes build floats and parade them through the city, throwing presents to the crowd – usually strings of colorful plastic beads or small toys.

2 **similar** *ähnlich*
3 **period** *Zeitraum*
3 **street parade** *Karnevals-zug*
6 **festivity** *Feierlichkeiten*
9 **to stretch** *sich erstrecken*
12 **to refer to sth** *auf etw. beziehen*
13 **to fast** *fasten*
15 **carnival float** *Karnevals-wagen*
16 **bead** *Perle*

The power of nature: Hurricane Katrina

Every year, the United States of America undergoes a hurricane season. Tropical cyclones build up over the North Atlantic Ocean and grow into hurricanes
20 or tropical storms which then make their way across the Atlantic to the American mainland. Tropical cyclone activity usually reaches its high point in the late summer as the water in the North Atlantic begins to warm up. In August 2005, the worst ever tropical cyclone hit the United States: Hurricane Katrina. More than 1,800 people died in the floods that followed. Hurricane Katrina started over the
25 Bahamas and then made its way over the Gulf of Mexico to Louisiana with winds of up to 175 miles/hour. The capital of Louisiana, New Orleans, was particularly badly hit by the hurricane. New Orleans is on the southern coast of the USA and part of the city is below sea level. The city is protected by a system of levees or dams which were designed for storms of Category 3. Hurricane Katrina, however,
30 was a Category 4 storm, and the levees broke, resulting in serious flooding. The floods did more damage to the city than the storm itself. About 80% of the city was under water. Although the Mayor of New Orleans called for an evacuation of the city in the days before the hurricane, thousands of people chose not to leave their homes for different reasons. Their decision to stay – though understandable
35 – also added to the problems of the emergency relief campaign.

18 **to undergo** *durchmachen*
19 **cyclone** *Wirbelsturm*
26 **particularly** *besonders*
28 **below sea level** *unter dem Meeresspiegel*
28 **protected** *geschützt*
28 **levee** *Damm*
31 **damage** *Schaden*
32 **mayor** *Bürgermeister*
32 **evacuation** *Evakuierung*
35 **emergency relief campaign** *Nothilfe*

Ziel: *Awareness*, Vorüberlegungen zum Thema *Forgiveness*
Der Titel *Forgiving Katrina* führt zunächst zu der falschen Annahme, mit dem Namen *Katrina* könnte ein Mädchen gemeint sein. **Aufgabe 1** unterstützt diese Annahme zusätzlich und bereitet so die Beschäftigung mit dem Ende der Geschichte vor.

Die SuS beschreiben zunächst für sich die geforderten Situationen. Anschließend tauschen sie sich in Dreier- oder Vierergruppen über ihre Ergebnisse aus (*Buzz Group*/Bienenkorb). Die Ergebnisse werden nicht noch einmal in der Klasse besprochen.

pre-reading
KV 2.1, Aufg.1a), 1b)
ca. 15 min.
Buzz Group

Ziel: Sicherung des Textverständnisses, Schreiben eines Zeitungsartikels
Aufgabe 2 sollte vor dem Hören/Lesen des Textes besprochen werden und während bzw. unmittelbar nach dem Hören/Lesen bearbeitet werden. Falls der Begriff *feature story* nicht bekannt ist, sollte er kurz erläutert werden:

> *A feature story, also called human-interest story, is a newspaper article or report which focuses on the "human aspects" of the event. It is designed to engage interest and arouse sympathy for the people, problems and situations.*

Die Ergebnissicherung erfolgt anschließend im Klassengespräch.

Unmittelbar an die Aufgabe 2 kann sich die folgende **Hausaufgabe** anschließen:

> *Write an article for a magazine that focuses on the "human interest" aspect of the story. Use the (parts of) sentences that you underlined.*

while-reading
KV 2.1, Aufg. 2
ca. 20–30 min.

Ziel: Auseinandersetzung mit dem Ende der Geschichte; kreatives Schreiben
Durchführung: Nach einer Murmelphase zur Ideenfindung (Aufgabe 3a) führen die SuS die Geschichte in einem Dialog (Aufgabe 3b) fort. Die Dialoge sind Ausdruck der Interpretation des Endes. Auf diesen Aspekt sollte im Feedback-Gespräch im Anschluss an die Vorträge der Dialoge eingegangen werden.

post-reading
KV 2.1, Aufg. 3
ca. 45 min.

Mögliche Erweiterung: Es kann sich eine Diskussion anschließen, ob die Worte *"I forgive you"* zwingend an Maurice gerichtet sein müssen. Denkbar wäre auch eine Interpretation, dass Sadie hier – wie im Titel angedeutet – dem Hurrikan *Katrina* vergibt, dass die Tatsache, dass sowohl Leben und Traditionen New Orleans, als auch ihr persönliches Leben weiter geht, sie *Katrina* akzeptieren lässt.

Erweiterung Klassenstufe 10 (ev. 9): Projektarbeit zum Thema *The political dimension of Hurricane Katrina* (KV 2.2).

KV 2.2

1. Forgiving

a) *What would you forgive your boyfriend or girlfriend for? Describe three situations that you could forgive.*

1. _____

2. _____

3. _____

b) *What wouldn't you forgive your boyfriend or girlfriend for? Describe three situations you wouldn't be able to forgive.*

1. _____

2. _____

3. _____

2. Listening / Reading: Forgiving Katrina

Underline sentences or parts of sentences in the story that could be used as ...

- the headline of a feature story about New Orleans after Katrina.
- parts of an article about New Orleans after Katrina.

3. Creative Writing:

At the end of the story Sadie says "I forgive you" to her boyfriend.

a) *Talk to your partner about the following questions and take notes.*

- What does she forgive him?
- Does he understand, why she says those words?
- Does he also feel he needs to be forgiven?
- How will he react?

b) *Now use your results to continue the story. Write a dialogue between Sadie and Maurice. Start like this:*

And as they stood there together and looked at the scenes of color and music around them,
Sadie finally spoke the three words she had been meaning to say for a long time. "I forgive you."

© Ernst Klett Sprachen GmbH, Stuttgart 2014 | www.klett.de | Alle Rechte vorbehalten
Kopieren für den eigenen Unterrichtsgebrauch gestattet.
ISBN 978-3-12-577343-X

Mardi Gras / Hurricane Katrina

Others from the neighborhood shared Sadie's opinion, and those who had come back to the city soon began to make preparations for Mardi Gras. They took their floats out of the garage and let them dry in the sun. They cut away the rotten wood, cleaned off the mold and repainted them. Some even created new designs which criticized the government's handling of the emergency. Too little, too late. Black America left to rot. At night, they sat together and made new costumes from old clothes.

(ll. 58–64)

Mardi Gras parades are not so unlike our German carnival parades in Cologne or Düsseldorf on Shrove Monday. The story hints at the fact that some of the floats had political topics – just like they do in Germany.

Group project: Work in groups of three!

Task 1.   Find out what the citizens of New Orleans criticized about how the American government handled the situation after Katrina. You can find a lot of interesting information on *http://en.wikipedia.org/wiki/Criticism_of_government_response_to_Hurricane_Katrina* and *http://en.wikipedia.org/wiki/Social_effects_of_Hurricane_Katrina.*

Use an extra sheet of paper and copy the following beginnings. Finish the sentences using the information you have gathered:

Hurricane Katrina caused a lot of damage in New Orleans, for example …

President Bush was criticized for his behavior during the crisis because he …

The Federal Emergency Management Agency, whose job it is to organize help in case of a disaster, was criticized heavily for …

The local government did not do a good job. They …

A lot of people talked of discrimination because …

Task 2.   *Imagine you are a member of a krewe in New Orleans after Katrina. What would be your political statement for the parade?*

a) Find a slogan. Describe the float you would like to build and draw a sketch of it.

OR

b) Design a costume you would like to wear at this particular Mardi Gras parade and draw a sketch of it. Describe the significance of your costume design. What does it stand for or mean?

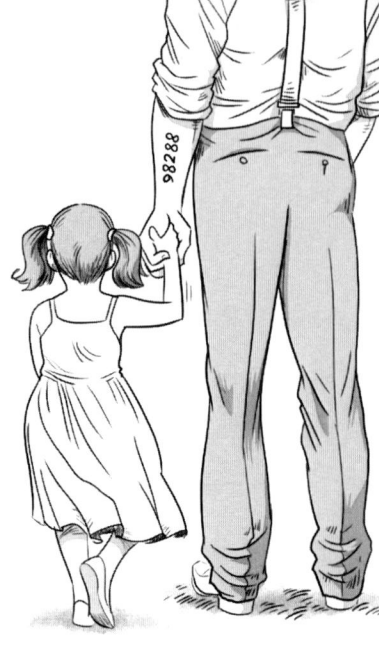

Opa Joe by David Fermer

Lucy peeled the apples and chopped them into small pieces. She ground some walnuts into a brown pulp. Then she added two tablespoons of cinnamon, a sprinkling of sugar and a drop of red wine. As she mixed the ingredients together she thought of the story this food had come to represent: the Exodus. The
5 *Charoset* – the dish she was preparing – was a symbol for the mortar the Jewish people once used as slaves when they were forced to make buildings for the Egyptian pharaohs. Everything in the Passover meal was symbolic for something.

Dusk was falling outside. Lucy could hear the sound of rush-hour traffic on Brooklyn Bridge as the front door opened and closed and the first guests arrived.
10 Family mainly, a few friends, neighbors, from eight months to eighty years old. The only person missing was Opa Joe.

It was the first time Lucy's family was celebrating Passover without him. Opa Joe had died only a few weeks ago, aged almost ninety. They called him "Opa Joe" because he was originally from Germany. He had come to America with his wife
15 in 1946. In all the years Opa Joe had been living in New York, he'd never lost his German accent. He always rolled his "r"s and pronounce his "v"s as a "w" and his "th" was more like a "d". He loved to speak German – much to the annoyance of Lucy's mother. Opa Joe said it was the most beautiful language in the world. And when Lucy's mother reminded him of what the Nazis once did to him and his
20 family, Opa Joe just shrugged his shoulders and said, "It is not their language that is to blame."

Opa Joe was a beacon of light in Lucy's life. Whenever she felt bad, whenever a cloud of gloom came over her, she went to visit him at his apartment in Crown Heights. "I have been to some dark places in my life," he would tell her. "I know
25 what it is to feel no hope, to think the world is a bad place. But life always goes on, *meydl*, even from the darkest point, even when you think there is no light at all. If you open your eyes and your heart, you will always find light somewhere."

It wasn't the first time that Lucy felt sad while preparing the Passover meal. It was a festival born of suffering. The six items of food on the Seder plate were
30 used to tell the story of the Exodus: the enslavement of the Jews in Egypt, their escape under the leadership of Moses, and the plagues which God inflicted on the Egyptian people. The Passover reminded the Jewish people of where they came from, the birth of a nation from the chains of suffering.

And now Lucy's mother had cancer. The doctors said she would be okay, that
35 her chances were good, but what if her mother died? Lucy had three younger brothers. The youngest was only eight! Lucy was in her last year of high school. She wanted to go to university, to study. But how could she go if her mother was sick?

Lucy put the *Zeroa* into the oven. Half-an-hour cooking time. The bone of meat
40 represented the mighty arm of God, the same arm that punished the Egyptians by killing their first-born children.

1 **to peel** *schälen*
1 **to chop** *klein schneiden*
1 **to grind (ground, ground)** *(zer)mahlen*
2 **pulp** *Brei*
2 **cinnamon** *Zimt*
5 **mortar** *Mörtel*
7 **Passover** *Passahfest*
8 **dusk** *Abenddämmerung*
16 **to pronounce** *aussprechen*
17 **annoyance** *Ärger*
20 **to shrug one's shoulders** *die Achseln zucken*
21 **to blame** *die Schuld geben*
22 **beacon of light** *Fels in der Brandung*
23 **gloom** *Hoffnungslosigkeit*
29 **suffering** *Leiden*
30 **enslavement** *Versklavung*
31 **plague** *Seuche*
31 **to inflict** *(Schaden) zufügen*
33 **chain** *Kette*
34 **cancer** *Krebs*
40 **mighty** *gewaltig*
40 **to punish** *bestrafen*

Lucy's father came into the kitchen. "Are you all right?"

"Everything is fine."

"Can I give you a hand?"

45 "Go back to your guests, Papa. Bring Mama fresh water." She gave her father a pitcher of water and pushed him out of the room. Next were the *Karpas*, potatoes in salt water to represent the tears of the Jews.

Later Lucy took the wine into the main room. The table was set with their best dishes and finest cutlery. The men were sitting in her father's study, talking in 50 quiet voices. Children were running around the table, laughing. Mothers stood at the window and looked out over East River. Lucy saw the vacant chair at the head of the table, the chair where Opa Joe had always sat. No one would sit in that chair today.

Lucy remembered the first time she saw the tattooed number on Opa Joe's 55 arm. She was with him at this table, a little primary school girl doing her homework with grandpa. For the first time he told her his story, the story of that terrible tattoo, of the concentration camp in Poland where he and his family had been sent during the war. "The world was a dark place when my parents died. I was nineteen. I felt no hope, saw no light. But then, one day, I caught sight of a face 60 among the inmates. A girl my age. She smiled at me, and I could see her eyes light up. That was your grandmother, Lucy. Then I knew everything would work out. That everything would be fine." And then he would recite a German poem and remind Lucy that even in the darkest hour there is always light.

As Lucy went back to the kitchen to finish the Seder plates, she wanted to cry. 65 She missed Opa Joe. She didn't want to have to miss her mother, too. Suddenly she felt overwhelmed by the suffering. Was there no end?

She took the meat out of the oven and added it to the five other items on the Seder plate. Six portions of food her father would later use to tell the story of the Exodus.

70 When Lucy carried the first two Seder plates into the main room, the front door opened and the new neighbors arrived: a family who had arrived from Israel the week before. Her father had immediately invited the new arrivals to the Passover Seder. Lucy had only seen the parents, but now she saw they had children, too. Two small girls and a boy about the same age as her, handsome, 75 with thick black hair and dark eyes. As the family came into the apartment, the boy looked down the hall and saw Lucy in the kitchen. He smiled and his eyes lit up, and suddenly Lucy's fear vanished, and she heard a voice whisper in her ear, the voice of Opa Joe. "Everything will be good, *meydl*. Everything will be good."

* * *

46 **pitcher** *Krug*
47 **tear** *Träne*
49 **dishes** *Geschirr*
49 **cutlery** *Besteck*
49 **study** *Arbeitszimmer*
51 **vacant** *frei*
60 **inmate** *Insasse*
61 **to work out** *gut ausgehen*
61 **to light up** *aufleuchten*
62 **to recite** *vortragen*
66 **overwhelmed** *überwältigt*
72 **immediately** *sofort*
72 **new arrivals** *Neuankömmlinge*
74 **handsome** *gut aussehend*
77 **to vanish** *verschwinden*

Passover: March/April

Passover is the name of a Jewish festival that is celebrated every year on the 15th day of the Jewish calendar month *Nisan*, which is usually in March or April. Because the USA has a large Jewish population, particularly in big cities like New York, Passover has become an important part of U.S. culture. Even non-Jews
5 *(gentiles)* know about it. The festival takes place over a period of eight days and celebrates the freeing of the Jewish people, the Israelites, from slavery in ancient Egypt. During Passover, the participants perform rituals which mirror the experience of their ancestors. They eat bitter herbs which represent the Israelites' bitter time of slavery and drink wine to celebrate their new freedom. The night
10 before Passover, Jewish families remove all food products that contain grain from their homes, because their ancestors had to leave Egypt so suddenly that they had to pack their bread before it was ready. The Seder is the name of the Passover feast which is eaten on the first two nights. The Seder follows fifteen steps and tells the story of the exodus from Egypt. The Hebrew word "seder" means *order*.
15 During the Seder, children also play an important role. The youngest child asks questions like "Why is this night different from all other nights?" The adults then answer with words from the *Haggadah*, a Jewish religious text. The telling of stories plays an important role in the Passover.

1 **Passover** *Passahfest*
3 **population** *Bevölkerung*
6 **slavery** *Sklaverei*
7 **participant** *Teilnehmer*
8 **ancestors** *Vorfahren*
8 **herbs** *Kräuter*
10 **to remove** *entfernen*
10 **to contain** *enthalten*
10 **grain** *Getreide*

Germans in the USA: The story of immigration

20 Germans were among the first immigrants to come to the USA in the 17th century to start a new life. Most of them were fleeing religious persecution in their home country. The main movement of German immigrants to the USA, however, took place in the 19th century. In the 1850s, following a potato famine in Germany, almost 1 million Germans immigrated to the United States. Another
25 700,000 came in the 1870s, and in the 1880s almost one and a half million Germans immigrated to the States. From 1850 to 1870, German was the most widely spoken language in North America after English. The German immigrants settled in the traditional "German belt" or the "German Triangle" which stretched from Minnesota to Missouri, across Illinois and Indiana, and into Ohio. There were so
30 many Germans in America that German immigrants found it difficult to integrate into society because they stuck with their own kind and could live and work in German. They founded German schools to maintain their language. The German Christmas later became the basis for many American Christmas traditions including the giving of presents, the Christmas tree and the emphasis on family.
35 German immigrants also introduced hot dogs and hamburgers into the American culture.

21 **persecution** *Verfolgung*
23 **famine** *Hungersnot*
28 **belt** *Gebiet*
31 **to stick with one's kind** *unter sich bleiben*
32 **to found** *gründen*
32 **to maintain** *erhalten*
34 **emphasis** *Schwerpunkt*

Ziel: Bewusstwerdung über eigene Erfahrungen mit Traditionen innerhalb der Familie und der eigenen Kultur

Die SuS tauschen sich über das Begehen von Feiertagen mit ihrem Nachbarn aus und lernen dabei auch kulturelle Unterschiede kennen.

pre-reading
KV 3.1, Aufg. 1
ca. 10 min.
ஃஃ

Ziel: Verständnissicherung

Die SuS hören den Text von CD und lesen gleichzeitig mit. Sie füllen die Tabelle in Einzelarbeit oder mit dem Partner aus. Danach werden die Ergebnisse im Klassenverband verglichen.

while-reading
KV 3.1, Aufg. 2
ca. 15–20 min.
◎

Ziel: Beschäftigung mit den zentralen Begriffen der Geschichte (z. B. *suffering, family, tradition*); Erkennen der inhärenten Textstruktur (Parallelität)

post-reading
KV 3.1, Aufg. 3, 4
ca. 30 min.
ஃஃ

1. Vertiefende Textarbeit durch Analyse *(why-questions)*

Die SuS füllen die Tabelle in Partnerarbeit aus und diskutieren die Warum-Fragen. Die Lösung der Tabelle kann z. B. als Overhead-Folie vorbereitet werden. Die Lösungen werden im Klassenverband besprochen.

2. Kreativer Umgang mit dem Text *(word clouds)*

Die SuS erstellen den Anweisungen folgend *word clouds*, drucken sie aus, kleben sie auf ihren Zettel und hängen sie an einer bereitgestellten Fläche auf. Es entsteht eine „Galerie". Anschließend betrachten sie die erstellten Produkte und wählen drei *word clouds* aus, die aus ihrer Sicht die Botschaft der Geschichte besonders gut ausdrücken, und begründen dies schriftlich oder mündlich.

Alternativ kann die Erstellung der *word clouds* auch als Hausaufgabe durchgeführt werden. Die Galeriebetrachtung erfolgt dann in der nächsten Stunde.

KV 3.2
ca. 30 min.
ஃஃ ⠀www.⟶
Fläche zum Aufhängen der Produkte, Heftzwecken oder Tesafilm, Internetzugang und Drucker notwendig!
Alternativ: Hausaufgabe

1. **Before you read the story:**

   Passover (or Pessach, as Jewish people call this important Jewish holiday) is a time of rituals and celebrations. Families spend this time together, eating the Seder meal together, remembering the past of their people and celebrating the freeing of the Jews from slavery in Egypt.

   Are there any traditions in your family, do you celebrate any (religious) festivals? What are these festivities like?
   Does the whole family gather together? What do you eat? Are there any rituals that have special meanings?
   Do you understand all the parts of these rituals?
   Tell your partner about these festivals and how you celebrate them.

2. **While you are reading / listening to the story:**

   Lucy is preparing the Seder meal. Make a list of the rituals:

name of the dish	food and how it is prepared	ritual meaning

3. **After you have read the story:**

   a) *There are many parallels between the history of the Jewish people and Opa Joe's life.*
      Describe the stations as you find out about them from the story:

The Story of Passover / the Exodus of the Jews	Opa Joe's Life Story
– enslavement of the Jews in Egypt	

   b) *The ending of this story leaves a lot of why-questions:*
      Lucy is very sad and worried while she is preparing the food for Passover. Why?
      Yet her fear vanishes in the end and she thinks everything will be OK. Why?
      And why does she have to think of Opa Joe at that moment?

Passover

Name: _____

This story draws a lot of parallels between the history of the Jews and the individual life story of Opa Joe, the suffering of a people and the suffering of two individuals, the meaning of religious symbols and their meaning for Lucy.

Sometimes it is easier to understand the main points of a story when we transform it into a different medium, e.g. a film or a song – in this case into a new art form: *a word cloud*.

Step 1: *Decide on a part of the story, a passage, a few sentences or even single words that you think are very important because they carry the "essence" or the gist of the story. Mark or highlight them in your text.*

Step 2: *Go to http://www.wordle.net/create. Type in the text that you have chosen.*

Step 3: *Create word clouds by pressing the "create" button. Repeat this step until you think the result shows what you consider important in this story. You can also change colors and fonts.*

Step 4: *Print out your result and glue it onto this worksheet.*

Step 5: *(optional): Choose an important festival from your own culture. Make a mind map. Use the words of this mind map to make your personal word cloud.*

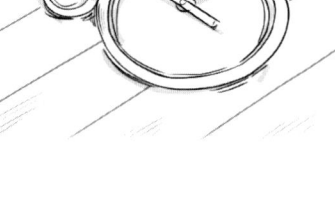

ABC by David Fermer

In the city that James Chen came from, he didn't feel different at all. San Francisco, on the Pacific Coast, is a true melting pot of cultures. It has (after New York City) the largest population of Chinese-Americans in the USA. They make up more than a fifth of the city's population. So seeing someone with black hair, light
5 brown skin and dark eyes was nothing special on the streets of "Frisco".

But then James' family moved to a small town in Wyoming. His father, an engineer, took on a three-year contract for the Sinclair Oil Corporation in Casper, a town of 50,000 people. James and his family were the only Asians in town.

James knew he looked Asian, but he didn't feel Asian at all. He spoke like an
10 American. He played baseball like an American. He listened to American music, wore the same clothes as all the other kids in high school, and had the same dreams. The fact that he was an "ABC", an American-born Chinese, wasn't important at all. But in Casper, things were different.

To make things worse, his first day at his new high school was April 1st. Back in
15 San Francisco, April Fool's Day wasn't a big thing. A few of the younger kids played dumb pranks, put whoopee cushions on their teacher's chair, pretended they had a terrible nosebleed (with fake blood) to get out of class. Harmless fun. But in Casper, April Fool's Day was a free ticket to test the new boy. And the person who decided to take on the job was Ryan, the biggest mouth (and the biggest bank
20 account) in the whole school.

Ryan decided to be James' best friend on his first day of school. He took James under his wing, showed him around, introduced him to other kids. In many ways it was the perfect start. James could see that being friends with Ryan was definitely a good thing. Everyone treated him with respect. Later he would find
25 out why.

But Ryan didn't really want to be friends with the new boy. He was just preparing the ground for his April Fool's Day prank. And as the saying goes: "The bigger they are, the harder they fall". Ryan just wanted to build James up before dropping him hard.
30 That same afternoon, when the 10th graders were outside doing track and field, Ryan slipped away, took James' keys from the changing room and went to his locker where he left a bag of the finest marihuana. Then he told Larry Lemond from the 7th grade to go to the principal's office and tell Mrs. Mullen that the new boy had offered to sell him and his friends drugs. Ryan's timing was perfect. As
35 he came back to the lockers twenty minutes later with James and the rest of the class, the school janitor was opening James' locker with a pair of bolt cutters while Mrs. Mullen, the principal, looked over his shoulder. When Mrs. Mullen reached into James' locker and pulled out the bag of weed, James had some explaining to do.

1 **different** *anders*
2 **melting pot** *Schmelztiegel*
3 **to make up** *ausmachen*
7 **contract** *Vertrag*
16 **prank** *Streich*
16 **whoopee cushion** *Furzkissen*
16 **to pretend** *vortäuschen*
17 **nosebleed** *Nasenbluten*
19 **bank account** *Bankkonto*
21 **to take sb under one's wing** *unter seine Fittiche nehmen*
24 **to treat** *behandeln*
28 **to build up** *aufbauen*
29 **to drop** *fallen lassen*
30 **track and field** *Leichtathletik*
31 **to slip away** *sich wegschleichen*
32 **locker** *Schließfach*
36 **janitor** *Hausmeister*
36 **bolt cutters** *Bolzenschneider*
38 **to reach** *greifen*
38 **weed** *Gras*

40 It took James a couple of weeks to find out who had played the prank on him, and by the time he confronted Ryan about it, Ryan was no longer even trying to be nice. Ryan didn't like James at all. He felt threatened by the new boy. James was a likeable guy, smart, sporty, down to earth. The girls liked him because they could talk to him. The teachers liked him because he worked hard. And people in town

45 soon made his family feel welcome. Everybody wanted to invite James' family around for a meal, because everybody wanted to be invited by James' family in return. Real Chinese food! Where else could you find that in Casper?

Kirsty liked James as well. She was in his class, and they soon became friends. And when, after a year at his new school, Kirsty said they should return the favor

50 and play an April Fool's prank on Ryan this time, James liked the idea. He'd never forgiven Ryan for the humiliating start in his new school. It had taken months for people to stop seeing him as the dangerous drug-dealing Asian kid from the Californian ghetto. Now it was time to pay Ryan back.

The sleeping pills which Kirsty and James gave Ryan that morning were extra-

55 strong and tasteless. James had gotten them from an online Chinese pharmacy and they dissolved several of them into Ryan's drink. By lunch, Ryan could hardly keep his eyes open. Linda, who Ryan had wanted to date for years, managed to get Ryan into the washroom before he passed out completely. There, Kirsty and James put him in a wheelchair, undressed him down to his underwear, and wrote

60 "Kiss My Ass" on his chest in permanent ink. Then they wheeled him into the hall, dragged him up onto the stage, and closed the curtains. The whole school was scheduled to meet there during 5th period in order to discuss plans for the forthcoming *Sports Day*.

After lunch, while the hall was filling with students, James slipped off behind

65 the curtains and took up position by the ropes. As Mrs. Mullen came onto the stage and began to speak, she didn't notice that the curtains were slowly opening behind her. Only when the first children saw Ryan sleeping in the wheelchair behind her, half-naked and tattooed, and they suddenly burst into laughter, did she stop talking. Soon all eyes were on the boy slouched in the position as James

70 and Kirsty had left him. By the time Mrs. Mullen turned around to wake him, the whole room was in stitches, laughing and pointing at the big-mouthed bully who had made so many lives miserable. But the laughter soon died when Mrs. Mullen's attempts to wake Ryan failed. First she shook him by the shoulders, then she slapped him around the face. No reaction. By the time she turned around and

75 screamed across the hall, "Somebody call an ambulance!" the joke was over. Ryan's lifeless body slipped off the wheelchair and fell to the ground. Everyone knew he was dead.

* * *

42 **threatened** *bedroht*
43 **smart** *intelligent*
43 **down to earth** *bodenständig*
49 **to return a favor** *sich revanchieren*
51 **humiliating** *erniedrigend*
54 **sleeping pill** *Schlaftablette*
56 **to dissolve** *sich auflösen*
58 **washroom** *Toilette*
58 **to pass out** *bewusstlos werden*
59 **wheelchair** *Rollstuhl*
60 **permanent ink** *unlöschbare Tinte*
61 **to drag** *schleppen*
62 **to schedule** *planen*
63 **forthcoming** *bevorstehend*
69 **slouched** *zurückgelehnt*
71 **to be in stitches** *sich totlachen*
71 **to point at** *auf jdn/etw. zeigen*
71 **bully** *Rüpel*
74 **to slap** *schlagen*
76 **to slip off** *herunterrutschen*

April Fool's Day: April 1ˢᵗ

April Fool's Day is not a national holiday in the USA. It's a special day when people play practical jokes on each other. It's difficult to say when the tradition of April Fool's Day started. Some historians say it goes back to the 16ᵗʰ century. In the Middle Ages, New Year's Day was celebrated on March 25ᵗʰ in most European
5 towns. In some parts of France, festivities around New Year lasted for a week and ended on April 1ˢᵗ. In the 16ᵗʰ century, France changed the date of New Year from March 25ᵗʰ to January 1ˢᵗ, but many people in the country continued to celebrate on March 25ᵗʰ because they either hadn't heard about the change or didn't believe it. It's said that April Fool's started then as many people made fun of those who
10 still celebrated New Year on the old date. Although the tradition started in France, it only became popular in England in the 18ᵗʰ century. Like many U.S. traditions, April Fool's Day was 'imported' to the USA by British immigrants. Today, pranks and hoaxes are played all over the world on April 1ˢᵗ. In 1957, the British television channel, the BBC, played the first national hoax. The news reported about Swiss
15 farmers who had started growing spaghetti on trees. Film material showed the farmers cutting the spaghetti off the trees. The BBC received hundreds of phone calls from viewers asking how to grow their own spaghetti.

2 **practical joke** *Streich*
5 **festivity** *Feierlichkeiten*
5 **to last** *andauern*
8 **to believe** *glauben*
11 **popular** *beliebt*
12 **prank, hoax** *Streich*
17 **viewer** *Zuschauer*

Asian communities in the USA

The USA has a large Asian community, that is, people who can trace their
20 ancestry to one or more countries in Asia. The Asian community in the USA is estimated at around 18 to 20 million people. Asian immigrants have been coming to the USA for centuries. The first Indians came with the British colonial rulers in the 18ᵗʰ century. Filipinos escaped from their Spanish colonial masters and also settled in North America. Many Chinese and Japanese people began immigrating
25 to the U.S. in the mid-19ᵗʰ century because of poor economic conditions at home. They hoped to find work in the land of plenty. Many of them worked as laborers on the great railroads which crossed America from coast to coast, or on sugar plantations. Most Asians settled in the western part of America, and soon people there began to feel threatened by the growing numbers of Asian immigrants.
30 This resulted in the first set of laws aimed at stopping Asians from coming to the States, in particular from China. Later, the war with Japan during the Second World War also created a difficult climate for many Asian Americans, in particular those of Japanese descent. But after the war, more and more Asians became naturalized citizens, and the Asian community is now well integrated into U.S.
35 society where Asian Americans enjoy a high level of education and professional status.

19 **to trace** *zurück-verfolgen*
20 **ancestry** *Abstammung*
21 **to estimate** *schätzen*
22 **ruler** *Herrscher*
23 **master** *Herr*
24 **to settle** *besiedeln*
25 **economic** *wirtschaftlich*
26 **the land of plenty** *das Lande der unbegrenzten Möglichkeiten*
26 **laborer** *Arbeiter*
29 **threatened** *bedroht*
30 **to aim** *zum Ziel haben*
31 **in particular** *insbesondere*
33 **descent** *Herkunft*
34 **citizen** *Staatsbürger*

Ziel: Vorentlastung; Austausch über eigene Erfahrungen
Der kurze Text *April Fool's Day: April 1st (ABC – Additional information)* wird in Einzelarbeit gelesen. Im Anschluss berichten die SuS über eigene oder erlebte Aprilscherze *(pranks)*. Sie beurteilen diese und unterteilen sie in *funny and fully acceptable, not really funny, distasteful* und *cruel and not acceptable*. Dabei ist es auch möglich, mit den SuS gemeinsam Kriterien aufzustellen, wie ein Scherz sein muss, um noch als Scherz zu gelten und ab wann ein Scherz zu weit geht.

pre-reading
April Fool's Day: April 1st
Klassendiskussion
ca. 10 min.

Ziel: Leseverstehen (ggf. Hörverstehen) eines unbekannten Textes
Die Geschichte wird von den SuS in Einzelarbeit gelesen, ggf. auch von CD vorgespielt. Dabei notieren sie eventuelle Fragen zum Textverständnis und zu Vokabeln. Diese werden anschließend von der Klasse geklärt.

while-reading
Klassendiskussion
⇔

Ziel: KV 4.1: Reflektion des Textes durch ein Rollenspiel, Kennenlernen von Aspekten des amerikanischen Rechtssystems; KV 4.2: Textsicherung
KV 4.1 und KV 4.2 werden von verschiedenen Gruppen parallel behandelt. Dies ist nötig, da die Gruppe *Jury* während der Vorbereitung des *trials* und die anderen Gruppen während der Urteilsfindung der Jury ohne Aufgabe sind.

post-reading
KV 4.1, KV 4.2
ca. 75 min.
ᗘᗘᗘ ⟨www,⟩
Internetzugang sinnvoll!

Durchführung des Rollenspiels:
Die SuS teilen sich in folgende Gruppen auf:
> **Gruppe 1**: Der Angeklagte und seine Verteidiger
> **Gruppe 2**: Die Staatsanwaltschaft
> **Gruppe 3**: Die Zeugen
> **Gruppe 4**: Die Jury
> **Einzelner Schüler oder Schülergruppe**: Richter/in
> (Es sollte darauf geachtet werden, dass diese Rolle von einem Schüler / einer Schülerin / einer Schülergruppe übernommen wird, der / die recht sicher in Englisch ist / sind. Die Gruppe der Richter braucht u. U. mehr Zeit zur Vorbereitung und muss deshalb die KV 4.2 ggf. schneller bearbeiten.)

Die Schülergruppen bereiten ihre Rollen entsprechend der Rollenkarten vor. Sie haben dafür 20 Minuten Zeit. Danach wird der Prozess gespielt. Anschließend zieht sich die Jury zur Beratung zurück. Sie haben dafür ebenfalls 20 Minuten Zeit. Während dieser Zeit bearbeiten die anderen Gruppen KV 4.2. Wenn die Jury zurückkehrt, wird der Prozess fortgeführt. Die Jury verkündet ihr Urteil und begründet dies. Der/die Richter/innen verkünden daraufhin den Urteilsspruch. Sie können diesen bereits vorbereitet haben oder sich zu diesem Zeitpunkt kurz beraten.

Hinweis für die Gruppen (besonders Richter und Jury):

> *Search the Internet for information; watch the trial scene of "To Kill A Mockingbird" or any other trial scene to find out the exact wording of what a judge must say.*

Mögliche Anschlussaufgabe Diskussion: *Have we reached a fair verdict?*
Hausaufgabe im Anschluss an KV 4.2:

> *As journalists you have collected a lot of background information on the case. Write an article about what happened. Don't forget to answer the 5 "W's".*

The Crime: General Information (USA)

Murder is an intentional killing that is a) unlawful (i.e. not done in self-defense or in a war situation) and b) committed with "malice aforethought" (intent to harm or kill or reckless disregard for life). *Examples: A wife goes into a store, buys a lethal dose of rat poison and puts it into her husband's tea.*

Voluntary Manslaughter (also called "heat of passion" crime) occurs, when a person is suddenly provoked and kills in the heat of passion. The killing may be intentional, but the killer did not have full control over their behavior because of their emotional agitation. *Example: A husband comes home unexpectedly and finds his wife in bed with another man, the man makes fun of him and the husband kills his wife's lover.*

Involuntary Manslaughter means that the killing was not planned, but happened because the killer was too careless and caused another person's death by reckless behavior. *Example: Somebody drives under the influence of alcohol and kills somebody in an accident.*

Please note, that the differences between these crimes can be subtle, differ from state to state and are not the same as in Germany. For more information visit:
http://www.nolo.com/legal-encyclopedia/homicide-murder-manslaughter-32637.html

Role play: A Trial

You need four groups and one or more student(s) who would like to be the judge(s).

Role card group 1: You are James Chen, the defendant, and his lawyers – You must decide:
a) Are you guilty of a crime (if yes, which one) or are you innocent, because it was an accident? How do you plead?   b) What is your line of defense? Who are your witnesses? Which evidence can help you (read the text)?   c) What are you going to ask the witnesses?

Role card group 2: You work for the prosecution – You must decide:
a) What crime is the defendant guilty of? Murder, voluntary manslaughter or involuntary manslaughter? How would you like to see him punished?   b) What is your line of argument? Who are your witnesses? Which evidence can help you (read the text)?   c) What are you going to ask the witnesses?

Role card group 3: The witnesses
Who are you? A student or a teacher? Are you a friend of the defendant or of the victim?   What did you see / hear / hear about? It is your job to give truthful testimony. Look into the text for possible witnesses (e.g. Mrs. Mullen, Kirsty, girls who liked James, some of his teachers, some of Ryan's friends.   As in real life, you are not allowed to invent anything, only use facts from the text.

Role card group 4: The Jury / Journalists:
Part 1: While the others are preparing the trial, you will be journalists and do KV 2.   *Part 2:* While the others are doing KV2, you will be the jury and decide on the defendant's guilt or innocence. As the jury it is your job to listen to all the testimony given and to review all the evidence presented. Then you have to decide whether or not the defendant is guilty. If yes, was it murder, voluntary manslaughter or involuntary manslaughter? Or was it an accident, which means the defendant is not guilty and can go free?

Role card: Judge(s)
It is your job to organize the trial, to summarize the main points, to talk to the jury, to announce the verdict. Prepare for your role by checking up a) the stages of a trial, b) the language judges use in court, c) the possible verdicts you could pass.

1. James

Find the information in the text and take notes:

a) Describe the differences between San Francisco and Casper. How do they affect James' life?

San Francisco:	James' life in San Francisco:
Casper:	James' life in Casper:

b) How does James see himself – as American or as Chinese? Find proof in the text.

James sees himself as _____ . You know this because the text says:	Line(s):

c) Look for information on his social background (e.g. poor / middle class / rich family, big city or small town kid, education etc.) and underline it in the text.

2. The people in Casper

a) What was the first reaction to James and his family? Take notes and give proof from the text.

b) How did the people of Casper feel about James and his family after a while? Take notes and give proof.

c) How do you think the people are going to react to what happened? Give reasons for your opinion.

	a) first reaction	b) after a while	c) possible reaction to what happened
Ryan			
other kids			
teachers/principal			
other people from Casper			

Escape to the USA by David Fermer

It's about 9 o'clock in the evening when darkness finally falls. We've been here for hours, waiting in the bushes, looking down to the canyon below.

In the distance we can hear the sound of the celebrations, music carried over to us by the southwesterly wind, like a call reminding us of our final destination.

5 It's *Cinco de Mayo*, May 5th, and Hispanics all across America are celebrating their cultural heritage.

But we are not celebrating with them. Not this year. We are like animals in a cage, waiting to escape. My father and I try not to breathe too loudly, even though our hearts are beating like the hooves of a galloping horse. They have been

10 beating madly since we got here, and I can't wait for this night to be over, when my heart can finally go back to its normal rhythm, when I can breathe freely, without being scared that someone will hear me.

For the moment it's the *banditos* we're scared of, the bandits. They're waiting for us down in that canyon, like vultures waiting for an animal to die. On the other

15 side of the dry riverbed is the U.S.-Mexico border. A patrol car occasionally passes, but everyone here knows that a 2,000-mile border can't be patrolled all the time.

There must be hundreds of people hiding around us in the bushes. Not just Mexicans; Hondurans and Guatemalans, too. People from El Salvador. People who've had family members killed by the drug cartels, or are victims of the

20 violence in Central America. People who have friends or family on the other side of the fence. People who have hope. Hope for a better future, with all the promise of the United States.

My father wanted me to come because I speak English. From a very young age I wanted to master the English language, as if somehow I knew one day I would

25 come to this country. Most Mexicans don't speak English. They don't want to. It's the language of the *gringos*, the Americans, our extra-large neighbor who, for too long, has bossed Mexico around. They can control our politicians and our businesses, but they cannot control the thousands of people trying to come into their country every day. Of the hundreds waiting in the bushes tonight, maybe

30 only ten will make it. The others will try again tomorrow, and the night after that, until they either give up or get caught by the *banditos*. The *banditos* prey on the weak. Women, children, the old. They steal their money, rape and murder. My father says he doesn't know who scares him more: the U.S. border control guards or the *banditos*. At least we know the Americans won't kill us.

35 We wait another three hours. We see fireworks on the U.S. side of the border. Explosions in green, white and red, the colors of the Mexican flag. When the fireworks have stopped, the people will make a run for it. When the first run, everybody runs. Our only chance is in numbers: the border patrol agents cannot stop *all* of us. Nor can the *banditos*.

3 **distance** *Ferne*
6 **heritage** *Erbe*
8 **cage** *Käfig*
8 **to escape** *fliehen*
9 **to beat** *klopfen*
10 **madly** *wie verrückt*
14 **vulture** *Geier*
15 **riverbed** *Flussbett*
15 **border** *Grenze*
15 **occasionally** *gelegentlich*
15 **to pass** *vorbeikommen*
19 **victim** *Opfer*
21 **fence** *Zaun*
24 **to master** *meistern*
27 **to boss around** *herumkommandieren*
31 **to catch** *fangen*
31 **to prey on** *Jagd machen*
32 **to rape** *vergewaltigen*
35 **fireworks** *Feuerwerk*

40 *"Suerte, mi hijo.* Good luck, my son", my father says to me as we see the first people moving out into the darkness. I look at my father and see sadness in his eyes. He has the same eyes as Miguel, my cousin, who is meeting us on the other side. Miguel has been in the States for years. He will bring us to safety. It was his idea that we make this dangerous journey. "Come on, *tío*," he told my father on

45 the phone. "You can find work in America. Everyone has a chance here."

But my father is not coming for himself. He is doing this for me, his *hijo gringo*, his American son. That's what he calls me because of my good English and my interest in American culture, and he thinks my future is in the United States. I am fourteen years old. Once I am in America – even as an illegal immigrant – I can go

50 to high school.

"Cuidado. Be careful", he says to me as we stand up and start to join the other shadows running through the night. I can't see any faces, but I can hear the people around me, their breath, their footsteps, the branches cracking under their feet.

55 Now we are running. We run for our lives. My father tries to hold my hand, but other people run between us and we get separated. I keep as close as I can, looking into the darkness around me, searching for danger signs, for the *banditos*. We make it to the fence. People fall to their knees and scramble under a hole cut out of the wire, the dust swirling around them like a hurricane. Still no lights.

60 Someone shouts from the canyon. A women screams. The *banditos* have caught their first victim.

"Rápido. Quickly." My father pushes me to the ground and kicks me through the hole in the fence. When I get to my feet on the other side, I look back, but he doesn't follow me. He just stays there, kneeling by the hole in the fence, tears in

65 his eyes. I know straightaway: he isn't coming.

"Papa …" I say, but he shakes his head. "Papa!"

"Corre, hijo. Corre. Run, my son, run. You know where you have to go. Live long. I love you. Your mother loves you, too."

Someone grabs my arm and pulls me away from the fence. "Run, boy, run."

70 Suddenly I'm getting dragged off and my father is getting smaller and smaller, swallowed by the darkness, and I want to cry out and say "no! no! no!" but I can't, because my feet are moving so fast over the dusty ground, and soon people start slowing down around me, taking deep breaths and laughing, and someone says "We made it!" and I can see warehouses in the distance and several cars start

75 their engines and I know my cousin, Miguel, is in one of those cars and that this is the beginning of a new life for me.

I look back to the fence one last time. I see nothing but darkness.

He did this for me, his *hijo gringo*, his American son.

* * *

43 safety *Sicherheit*
51 to join *sich anschließen*
52 shadow *Schatten*
53 breath *Atmen*
53 branch *Zweig*
56 separated *getrennt*
57 sign *Zeichen*
58 to scramble *sich durch etw. zwängen*
59 wire *Draht*
59 dust *Staub*
65 straightaway *sofort*
69 to grab *schnappen*
70 to drag off *wegziehen*
71 to swallow *schlucken*
73 to take a deep breath *tief einatmen*
74 warehouse *Lagerhaus*

Cinco de Mayo: May 5th

Cinco de Mayo means "May 5th" in Spanish, the main language in Central and Southern America, and the second most important language in the United States of America, where over 30 million people of Mexican descent live. Cinco de Mayo is an annual festival which celebrates Mexico's victory over France at the Battle
5 of Puebla on May 5th, 1862. Cinco de Mayo has nothing to do with Mexican Independence Day. In fact, Cinco de Mayo is not a Mexican holiday at all. It is celebrated by Mexican-Americans and virtually ignored in Mexico. It was started in the 19th century by Mexican-American communities in California who wanted to celebrate their Mexican heritage and was only officially recognized by the U.S.
10 government as a national holiday in 2005. The celebrations are full of traditional Mexican symbols such as the Virgin de Guadalupe and Mexican music, as well as Mexican food such as guacamole and tortilla chips. The largest Cinco de Mayo party takes place every year in Los Angeles, California, but other cities such as Denver, New York, Phoenix and Houston all have big celebrations, too.

3 **descent** *Abstammung*
4 **annual** *jährlich*
4 **victory** *Sieg*
7 **virtually** *praktisch*
9 **heritage** *Erbe*
9 **recognized** *anerkannt*
13 **to take place** *stattfinden*

Secret lives: Illegal immigration in the USA

Every year, thousands of people come into the United States illegally in the hope of finding a better future. Most of them are looking for better employment opportunities there. Others are escaping political oppression or violence in their home land. Most of them enter the country by illegally crossing the U.S.-Mexico
20 border which is more than 3,000 kilometers long. It is estimated that over 11 million people live in the USA illegally, over half of them come from Mexico. Every year, more people try to enter the U.S. illegally than legally, and the U.S. Border Patrol apprehends more than 300,000 people on the U.S.-Mexico border. A similar number of immigrants manages to get past the border patrols successfully every
25 year. People wanting to cross the border illegally often hire professionals who help them. These people, who smuggle illegal immigrants across the border for money, are known as "coyotes". Most of the immigrants who come into the USA illegally plan to go back to their home country after having earned some money. However, the increased costs of hiring "coyotes" to smuggle people into the
30 country have resulted in a lower return rate, as illegal immigrants stay in the U.S. for longer periods to pay off their debts. Some illegal immigrants have been living in the USA for years. They are fully integrated into American society, but are still "illegal". Many people think long-term illegal immigrants should be given a U.S. passport so that they can live and work as normal American citizens.

17 **employment opportunities** *Arbeitsmöglichkeiten*
18 **oppression** *Unterdrückung*
20 **border** *Grenze*
20 **to estimate** *schätzen*
23 **to apprehend** *festnehmen*
23 **similar** *ähnlich*
29 **increased** *gestiegen*
30 **rate** *Quote*
31 **debts** *Schulden*
33 **long-term** *Langzeit-*
34 **citizen** *Staatsbürger*

Ziel: *Awareness,* Nachdenken über das Leben von Immigranten

Aufgabe 1: Die SuS erstellen eine persönliche Liste von Dingen, die sie vermissen würden, wenn sie ihr Leben komplett aufgeben müssten (z. B. um in einem anderen Land zu leben) und vergleichen diese anschließend mit der Liste ihres Nachbarn.

pre-reading
KV 5.1, Aufg. 1
ca. 5 min.

Ziel: Textverständnis, Detailverständnis

Aufgaben 2 und 3 a): Im Anschluss lesen / hören die SuS den Text und tragen die Informationen, die sie dem Text entnehmen, ein. Partnerarbeit ist möglich. Anschließend werden die Lösungen im Klassenverband besprochen.

while-reading
KV 5.1, Aufg. 2, 3a)
ca. 15–20 min.

Ziel: persönliche Auseinandersetzung mit dem Thema „(illegale) Einwanderung"

Aufgabe 3 b): Die SuS diskutieren – vermutlich kontrovers – welche Risiken eine Flucht birgt, aus welchen Gründen illegale Einwanderer sie dennoch immer wieder unternehmen und ob sie selbst diese Risiken eingehen würden. Sie wägen Für und Wider ab. Anschließend werden die Ergebnisse im Plenum vorgestellt.

post-reading
KV 5.1, Aufg. 3b)
ca. 15–20 min.

Die **Aufgaben 4** und **5** sollen den SuS einen persönlicheren Zugang zur Situation der Charaktere unter deutlicher Bezugnahme auf die Geschichte näher bringen. Die SuS bereiten die Aufgaben in Partnerarbeit vor. Anschließend werden die Resultate im Plenum besprochen. Dabei sollte, wo möglich, ein Bezug auf die Details der Geschichte hergestellt werden.

KV 5.2, Aufg. 4, 5
ca. 20–25 min.

Ziel: Ergebnissicherung, Kreativität

Aufgabe 6 eignet sich gut als Hausaufgabe, denn sie bündelt die Ergebnisse der Stunde. Die SuS erfassen die wesentlichen Aspekte der Geschichte und setzen sie in eine Zeichnung um.

KV 5.2, Aufg. 6

Erweiterung: Kreative Aufgabe (optional)

Take the first four paragraphs of the story and turn them into a film. What would the first scenes be like? Make a storyboard.

Das *storyboard* kann für jeweils jede Szene eine einfache Tabelle mit 3 Spalten sein. Die Spalten haben folgende Überschriften:

Folie der Storyboard-Vorlage, DIN-A3-Papier
ca. 90 min.

Spalte 1: *Sketch of the scene (what you can see)*
Spalte 2: *Camera shots, angles, movements, lights*
Spalte 3: *Text / music / sounds*

Diese sprachlich und inhaltlich anspruchsvolle Aufgabe hilft den SuS, zusätzlich zu den Details auch die Atmosphäre der Geschichte zu erfassen und sie in ein visuelles Medium zu überführen. Es ist möglich, diese Aufgabe in arbeitsteiliger Gruppenarbeit zu organisieren, wobei jede Gruppe eine Szene übernimmt. Die Würdigung dieser Arbeit kann dann durch eine Präsentation und Aushang in der Klasse erfolgen.

1. Leaving your home

Before you read the story: Imagine you had to give up your whole old life – which five things would you miss most?

1. _____   4. _____

2. _____   5. _____

3. _____

2. Now read the story and take notes about the main character's lives and the situation they are in:

Time: _____   Place: _____

Father:	Son:	Cousin:

3. Why they flee:

a) Look at the advantages and risks of illegally escaping into the USA and make two lists. Also give the lines, where you found this information in the text.

advantages of an escape	risks of an escape:
	– danger of being caught by the U.S. border control guards (l. 15)

b) Get together into groups of three or four and discuss whether an escape is really worth the risks. Present your result and your reasons to the class.

4. Father and son:

At the end of the story, the father leaves his son behind and does not follow him into the United States. He tells him that he and his mother love him. Can that be true? Can you understand the father / the parents? Which alternatives have they got? Discuss these questions with a partner and take notes.

We think, the parents love / do not love their son because _____

_____

_____

We can / cannot understand the father because _____

_____

_____

5. Leaving your home, again

Go back to the list you made before reading the story (task 1). If you were in this same situation – would you make any changes to your list? Why / why not? What would you change?

6. Book cover

Imagine this story was the first chapter of a book titled *Hijo gringo – American son*. Draw an interesting book cover.

Divided Country by David Fermer

Tyler and Logan loved playing soldiers. They'd been friends all their lives and had started play fighting at a very young age. They made guns out of wood and shiny swords from aluminum foil and found old grey and blue clothes which they cut and stitched into hats and jackets.

5   Logan's great-great-great grandfather on his mother's side had been a soldier in the Confederate Army during the Civil War, so Logan, too, chose to dress up in the gray colors of the South. Tyler's descendants had been supporters of the Union, key players in making sure the border state of Kentucky, where the boys still lived today, stayed on the government's side. So when the time came to act

10   out the Civil War, Tyler put on the dark blue of the North.

They fought battles in each other's backyards, set up tents in the woods outside Fulton, crossed streams until their boots and pants were wet and sodden, hunting each other down like trappers before engaging in bloody combat.

"Come out, you Yankee coward!" Logan would shout when he'd cornered Tyler

15   in the woods. "Get your gray butt outta there!"

"Over my dead body!" Tyler would answer.

And Logan would beat his way through the bushes with his toy sword and trap Tyler, and the two boys would wrestle each other to the ground, shouting insults and playing strong and then hurt, until one of them was victorious. They

20   never argued about who was going to win. Their fights were always fair, the number of defeats and victories equal on both sides. It was as if Tyler and Logan had a secret agreement: they could both win battles, but neither of them would ever win the war.

It was on the last Monday in May, when the boys were about twelve, that they

25   decided to honor Memorial Day, that special day when Americans remembered the men and women who had died fighting for their country, with a special re-enactment of the Battle of Gettysburg. After their families had been to the cemetery to lay flowers on the graves of fallen soldiers, the boys put on their dirty uniforms and marched out to the woods where they came across something that

30   put an end to their childish games. They hadn't even started fighting when Tyler's foot disappeared into the ground and the boy fell over, banging his head against a tree. Tyler didn't cry – neither boy ever cried – although his face hurt badly. After Logan had helped him back onto his feet, they looked down into the hole – a hollow, empty space like a small cave, and Logan cried "Holy cow!" when he saw

35   what was inside: a human skull, black and skinless, and the whale-like bones of a rib cage. And resting on the bones was a rusty sword, blackened around the handle. The boys recognized it immediately. It was an officer's sword from the Civil War.

For a while they just stared down into the grave as if spellbound until Tyler

40   eventually said, "We'd better tell our parents."

3 **sword** *Schwert*
4 **to stitch** *nähen*
6 **civil war** *Bürgerkrieg*
7 **descendant** *Nachkomme*
8 **border** *Grenze*
9 **to act out** *nachspielen*
11 **backyard** *Garten hinter dem Haus*
11 **woods** *Wald*
12 **stream** *Bach*
12 **sodden** *durchnässt*
13 **to hunt** *jagen*
13 **to engage in bloody combat** *sich blutige Auseinandersetzungen liefern*
14 **coward** *Feigling*
14 **to corner** *in die Enge treiben*
15 **butt** *Hintern*
15 **outta** *out of*
18 **to wrestle** *ringen*
19 **insult** *Beleidigung*
19 **victorious** *siegreich*
21 **equal** *gleich*
22 **agreement** *Vereinbarung*
22 **battle** *Schlacht*
25 **to honor** *in Ehre halten*
26 **re-enactment** *Wiederaufführung*
28 **cemetery** *Friedhof*
28 **grave** *Grab*
29 **to come across** *auf etwas stoßen*
34 **hollow** *hohl*
35 **skull** *Schädel*
36 **rib cage** *Brustkorb*
39 **spellbound** *gebannt*

"What for?" Logan replied. "They'll only make us hand it over to the cops."

"Maybe they'll give us a reward."

"Maybe they won't. We should sell it ourselves. There are collectors out there who'd pay a lot of money for a sword like this."

45 "I don't know ..." Tyler said. "I think we'd better tell someone."

"You chicken!"

"Who you callin' a chicken?" Tyler pushed Logan by the shoulders, almost knocking him to the ground. "I found it! I decide what to do!"

"You didn't find nothin'! You just fell over."

50 "Well, whose foot was it that went into the grave? That sword belongs to me!"

"You cheatin' Yankee! You just wanna sell that sword on your own!"

"Now that's a good idea!" Tyler said. "Maybe I'll do just that!"

The two boys stood tall in front of each other, their eyes locked, their chests raised like pumped up tires, waiting for the other to strike. Who was going to

55 make the first move?

"What are we doin' here?" Logan said after a while. "We're fightin' over some old sword!"

"We ain't fightin' yet," said Tyler who was still clenching his fists.

"I don't wanna fight you, Tyler. Brother don't fight brother. Not no more."

60 The mention of the word "brother" seemed to disarm Tyler entirely. It was a phrase they had heard in school. "Brother against brother". That was the real tragedy of the American Civil War.

But that was then. This was now. Logan was right.

"Whaddya say we find out how much the sword's worth first?" Tyler suggested.

65 "Then we go to the police and tell 'em about it. See what they give us."

"Sounds like a plan." Logan held out his hand. "Shake on it."

And that's just what they did. They took the sword home, took some photos, put them on the Net, and – after seeing what some crazy people around the country were willing to pay for it – sold it to the highest bidder. $3,000. Not bad

70 for a couple of twelve-year-old boys. Feeling good-hearted, they donated 300 bucks to the City of Fulton. They split the rest 50/50. Their parents never did find out where the money came from. And, after it was all over, the two friends decided to put away their gray and blue uniforms, and their wooden guns and aluminum swords, and promised, as long as they lived, never to fight each other ever again.

41 **to hand sth over** *etw. übergeben*
42 **reward** *Belohnung*
43 **collector** *Sammler*
46 **chicken** *Weichei*
51 **to cheat** *betrügen*
51 **wanna** *want to*
38 **eyes locked** *direkt in die Augen sehen*
54 **tire** *Reifen*
54 **to strike** *zuschlagen*
58 **ain't** *are not*
58 **to clench one's fist** *die Faust ballen*
60 **to disarm** *entwaffnen*
64 **whaddya** *what do you*
66 **let's shake on it** *Hand darauf*
69 **bidder** *Bieter*
70 **good-hearted** *gutherzig*
70 **to donate** *spenden*
71 **buck** *Dollar*
71 **to split** *teilen*

Memorial Day: Last Monday in May

Memorial Day is a federal holiday in the United States and takes place every year on the last Monday in May. On Memorial Day, people remember the men and women who died while serving their country in war. Originally it began as a way to commemorate the soldiers who died in the American Civil War (1861 –
5 1865) and was known as "Decoration Day". More lives were lost in the American Civil War than in any other war in U.S. history. But in the 20th century, Memorial Day was extended to include all Americans who died while in military service. Traditionally, Americans go to cemeteries on Memorial Day, often placing American flags over the graves of dead soldiers. The biggest Memorial Day
10 parade takes place in Washington D.C. where thousands of people and celebrities come together to remember the fallen soldiers. Memorial Day also marks the unofficial start of the summer vacation period.

1 **to take place** *stattfinden*
3 **to serve** *dienen*
4 **to commemorate** *gedenken*
8 **cemetery** *Friedhof*
9 **grave** *Grab*
10 **celebrity** *Promi*

Brother against brother: The American Civil War

15 The American Civil War, fought between the southern and the northern states of the USA from 1861 to 1865, was the bloodiest war in U.S. history. Although the states in the south didn't have as much industry as the north, they had huge cotton plantation farms which produced masses of cotton for export. The cotton farm owners were rich and they controlled the south. The cotton farms used
20 slaves, which made profits even larger. During this period, the United States was still expanding to the west. Large parts of what now belongs to the United States were not yet part of the Union and many of the big cotton farmers feared that the process of expansion would bring about even bigger plantations in the west – and greater competition. So when the central government in Washington D.C.
25 called on the southern states to help pay for the costs of expansion, and also to abolish slavery, the 11 southern states broke away from the rest of the United States and created their own country called the Confederate States of America or the "Confederacy". The Confederacy didn't want to abolish slavery or pay for the building of the railways to the west. The remaining 25 states of the north called
30 themselves the Union. The army of the Union was nearly twice the size of the Confederate army. In the first few battles, neither side had military uniforms, which made it difficult to know who the enemy was. Later the Union started to wear blue uniforms and the Confederates gray coats. While many of the men who fought for the Confederate army knew how to fire a gun, most of the men in the
35 Union army worked in factories and had never fired a gun in their lives. Because of this, and despite the imbalance of money and manpower between north and south, the war went on for four years until the Confederates finally surrendered in Virginia. *The Battle of Gettysburg* in 1863 was the bloodiest battle in the war and is often described as the turning point in the conflict.

15 **civil war** *Bürgerkrieg*
18 **cotton plantation** *Baumwollplantage*
21 **to expand** *ausdehnen*
22 **to fear** *fürchten*
23 **expansion** *Erweiterung*
26 **to abolish** *abschaffen*
29 **remaining** *restlich*
30 **twice** *doppelt*
33 **coat** *Mantel*
34 **to fire** *schießen*
36 **despite** *trotz*
36 **imbalance** *Ungleichgewicht*
37 **to surrender** *kapitulieren*
39 **turning point** *Kriegswende*

Ziel: *Awareness*, Vorentlastung zweier Aspekte

Aufgabe 1: Die SuS entscheiden sich für eine der beiden Aufgaben, a) oder b) und besprechen diese mit ihrem Partner.

Aufgabe a) „Finders keepers, losers weepers" ist ein Kinderreim(!), der bedeutet, dass man behalten darf, was man findet. Hier werden zwei Aspekte der Geschichte vorweg genommen: 1. Es geht hier um Kinder, die etwas finden und 2. sollte hier kurz thematisiert werden, ob es wirklich legitim und legal ist, einen Fund einfach zu behalten. Die Frage wird am Ende wieder aufgegriffen und anhand der Geschichte konkret diskutiert, d. h. an dieser Stelle geht es nur um eine allgemeine Betrachtung.

Aufgabe b) lädt dazu ein, an andere geteilte Länder zu denken bzw. die Assoziationen zu einem ehemals geteilten Deutschland nicht auszuschließen, um dann wahrzunehmen, dass ein Land nicht nur durch eine Mauer geteilt werden kann. Hier kann sich möglicherweise eine kurze, historische Beschäftigung mit dem amerikanischen Bürgerkrieg anschließen, z. B. in einer Hausaufgabe. Diese Aufgabe ist anspruchsvoller als Aufgabe 1a); sie richtet sich eher an politik-/geschichtsinteressierte SuS und ist zur Differenzierung geeignet (siehe Aufgabe 4!).

> **Hausaufgabe**: *The American Civil War: Who fought whom, and why? How did it end?*

Im Anschluss lesen/hören die SuS den Text.

Ziel: Textverständnis, Vokabelarbeit

Aufgabe 2: Die SuS finden die in Aufgabe 2 definierten Wörter im Text und tragen sie in das Kreuzworträtsel ein. Partnerarbeit ist möglich. Anschließend werden die Lösungen im Klassenverband besprochen.

Ziel: *Awareness*, Auseinandersetzung mit eigenen Spielen, Jungen-/Mädchen-Interessen an der Geschichte

Aufgabe 3: Die Geschichte richtet sich möglicherweise mehr an Jungen, als an Mädchen. Diese Aufgabe gibt beiden Geschlechtern die Möglichkeit, einen eigenen, möglicherweise geschlechtsspezifischen Zugang zu einer Geschichte zu finden, die ihnen auch kulturell vermutlich eher fremd ist. An den Austausch mit dem Partner sollte sich unbedingt eine Klassendiskussion anschließen.

Ziel: vertieftes Textverständnis, Anschluss an Aufgabe 1

Aufgabe 4 greift die Lösungen aus Aufgabe 1 wieder auf und führt diese an der Geschichte fort. Für Aufgabe 4b) ist ein gewisses Vorwissen um die ehemalige Teilung Deutschlands aus dem Geschichts-/Politikunterricht nötig, ggf. brauchen die SuS Hilfe von der Lehrkraft.

Ziel: Weiterführende Projektarbeit (optional)

Die KV 6.2 bietet drei verschiedene Optionen zur Projektarbeit zum Thema *Memorial Day* an.

(Seitenrand-Hinweise:)

pre-reading
KV 6.1, Aufg. 1
ca. 5 min.
Differenzierungsmöglichkeit!

post-reading
KV 6.1, Aufg. 2
ca. 20–30 min.

KV 6.1, Aufg. 4
ca. 25 min.

KV 6.2
ca. 90 min.
DIN-A3-Papier, großes Posterpapier, dicke Stifte
Internetzugang für alle SuS nötig!

1. **Before you read the story choose one of the following two tasks. Work with a partner and take notes on your ideas. Keep these notes, you will need them again after you have read the story!**
   a) There is an English saying: *"Finders keepers, losers weepers."* What do you think it means? Is there a German saying with a similar meaning?

   OR

   b) The title of the story you are about to read is *Divided Country*. What are your associations / thoughts / feelings when you read this title? What might this story be about?

2. **After you have read the story, find the following words in the text. They all belong to the word field "war".**

Across →:
2. graveyard (AE)
4. dead (soldier)
6. a type of weapon
7. soldiers walk this way
8. a place where a dead person is buried
9. at Gettysburg there was a famous …

Down ↓:
1. the opposite of victory
2. a war between groups of people in the same country
3. clothes soldiers wear
5. fighting, especially during a time of war

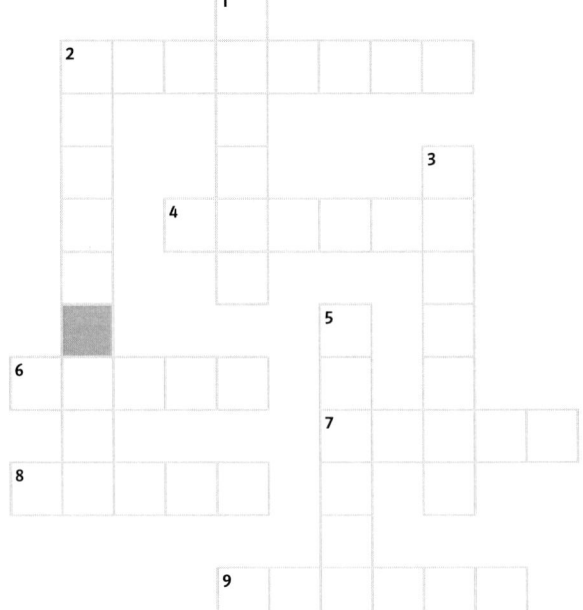

3. **Please work with a partner. If possible, boys should work with other boys, girls should work with girls.**
   Tyler and Logan love to pretend to be soldiers and to fight each other. Think of the games you played when you were younger. Now think of the story. Talk to your partner and take notes on the following questions:

   • In what way were / are your games different from the games these two twelve-year-olds play?
   • Why do you think your childhood games were different from Logan and Tyler's games?

4. **Look back at your notes from the first task.**
   If you did task 1 a):
   In the end the two boys briefly discuss some options of what to do with the sword they found.
   a) Come up with at least two options of what they could have done. What would have happened?
   b) Is the boys' solution morally and / or legally correct? Do you agree with it? Does the fact that they donate $300 to the City of Fulton make it better? What would you have done in their place? Say why.

   If you did task 1 b):
   Compare in which way Germany and America were both "divided" countries and how the people deal with this part of their history. Do you feel about it the same way these two boys do?

Memorial Day

Projects on the issues of *Memorial Day* and *fallen soldiers / war victims*:
*Choose **one** of the following tasks and create your own DIN A3 sheet (if you are doing this project on your own) or wall paper display (if you are working with a partner or as a group).*

1. **Project 1:**

   As you have read, the United States of America have a special day to commemorate their soldiers who have died in one of their wars. Did you know that Germany has a special day like that, too? It is called *"Volkstrauertag"*.
   Find out about its history and when and how it is celebrated. Discuss, whether this day should be kept or maybe replaced by something else? Either way, make suggestions how it should be observed in your opinion.

2. **Project 2:**

   How does this picture make you feel? What does it express? Maybe you can also listen to the song
   The universal soldier. (http://www.youtube.com/watch?v=A50lVLtSQik)
   Collect your thoughts, feelings and associations in a mind map.
   Then let this picture (or another one you may find on this topic) inspire you to write a poem.

3. **Project 3:**

   In Germany the issue of honoring soldiers is discussed in a rather controversial way which is often reflected in the way we deal with war memorials. Find out about war memorials in your city / town / area (e.g. on this website *http://www.denkmalprojekt.org/index.htm*).

   a) *Find out which war memorials there are; find out about details and if there has been a controversy about their existence.*
   b) *Discuss if you agree with the idea of putting up memorials to fallen soldiers.*
   c) *If you had to put up a memorial, who would it honor? What would it look like? What would the inscription say? Draw a rough sketch of it to explain your ideas.*

Freedom by David Fermer

Time stops in prison. There are no days of the week, no weekends, no holidays, no night and day. Seeing the sky once a day is the only reminder of life outside of the penitentiary walls. Each day you wait for night to fall, wait for time to pass faster in that blissful state of sleep. Feeling nothing is the best thing you can feel
5 in prison.

I was sentenced to three years in Dayton Correctional Institution for armed robbery, my first conviction as an adult, but they're letting me out after nineteen months. That's one month for every year of my life.

When the corrections officer calls out my name that morning, the morning of
10 the Fourth of July, I know this is the day I'm getting out. I can't help seeing the irony of it. Freedom on Independence Day. They couldn't have picked a finer occasion!

The CO takes me out of my block. My friends clap and cheer as I walk out of the gate. "Yo, brother! Send us a postcard from outside! You know our address!"
15 I count five gates on the way to the reception, past death row, past solitary, past the visiting area. The CO unlocks and locks each gate with methodical precision. When we get to the reception area, he takes off my handcuffs. The woman behind the counter gives me a box and wishes me good luck. The CO takes me into a small room and leaves me there. Inside the box are the clothes I
20 was wearing when I got here. My watch. My necklace. My wallet. That's all I have in the world.

I change into my old clothes, fold my orange prison uniform and leave it on the table. I didn't tell anyone I'm coming out today. There is no one to tell. The only people I know were here in the can with me.
25 The CO takes me to the front gate. "I hope I never see you again," he says with a hardened smile, and I know it's not the first time he's made this joke. We all know nearly half the released prisoners re-offend within the first three years.

I take the bus to town and get out at Jefferson Avenue. I see the gas station on the corner as the bus pulls away. On the other side of the road is the mall. I go
30 inside and find a toy store. I buy what I need, then I go back to the gas station. Cars are pulling in and out every few seconds. The gas station is located at a prime site, right on the junction between town and the freeway. They must make thousands of dollars a day.

I look past the rows of gas pumps to the store at the back. The fat lady is
35 working the cash register, the same lady who was here when Eezi, Jay and I held up the place. She was the one who set off the alarm before we even entered the store. She saw us coming. We didn't really have a plan. Eezi said it would be – well – easy, but that's why we call him Eezi. "Easy" is his favorite word. Jay said he'd done another gas station on the other side of town and there was nothing
40 the cops could do about it. We had guns, we had masks. Who cares about cameras?

3 **penitentiary** *Gefängnis*
4 **blissful** *glückselig*
6 **to sentence** *verurteilen*
6 **armed robbery** *bewaffneter Raubüberfall*
7 **conviction** *Verurteilung*
9 **corrections officer (CO)** *Gefängnisaufseher*
12 **occasion** *Anlass*
15 **death row** *Todestrakt*
15 **solitary** *Einzelhaft*
17 **handcuffs** *Handschellen*
20 **necklace** *Halskette*
24 **in the can** *hinter Gittern*
27 **to release** *freilassen*
27 **to re-offend** *erneut straffällig werden*
28 **gas station** *Tankstelle*
29 **to pull away** *davonfahren*
31 **located** *gelegen*
32 **junction** *Anschlussstelle*
32 **freeway** *Autobahn*
35 **cash register** *Registrierkasse*
35 **to hold up** *überfallen*

Klett

But Eezi was wearing a brand new pair of Nike Yeezys which the cops must have seen on the CCTV cameras. They asked some questions around the local shoe stores the next day and found the clerk who sold him the shoes. Eezi even filled out a coupon for a sweepstake, so the clerk had his name and address. The

45 cops picked him up an hour later. Jay and I were with him at the time. The money from the gas station, too.

Game over.

I watch the cars for a while as they pull into the station and fill up their tanks. Families, most of them. Kids on the back seat. No school for them today. Not on

50 the Fourth of July. They're loving it.

I think of my parents. We never once sat in a car together. Dad left when I was a kid, Momma got into drugs. I was in and out of schools all my life. Stopped going altogether when I was twelve. Started dealing when I was fifteen. Did my first stint in Juvenile when I was sixteen. Another when I was seventeen. Third

55 time lucky.

The fat lady takes a break and goes into the back room. She comes out a few minutes later with a coffee in her hand, back in time to serve the next customer. I take out the toy gun I bought at the kid's store and head for the door. The fat lady looks up from the register as the customer leaves and I step into the store.

60 She recognizes me straightaway. Her hand goes straight for the alarm under the counter.

"Whaddya want?" she asks as I walk up to her, the gun in my hand.

"I wanted to say sorry."

"Sorry?"

65 "Yeah. Sorry. For what we did to you. I am. Really. Sorry."

"That's okay ..." she stammers, her panicked eyes fixed on the gun in my hand. "We all do dumb things when we're young."

I point the toy gun at her. "D'you press the button already?"

"I ... yes ..." She looks out the window. A patrol car comes speeding into the

70 gas station, its blue sirens screaming.

"Then you'd better give me the money, ma'am."

The fat lady opens the register and starts taking out the cash.

"Don't worry, it's not real," I tell her as I take the money and put the toy gun down on the counter. Two cops are waiting for me outside, guns drawn. They

75 scream at me as I step out of the store. I drop the cash, put my hands behind my head and wait for them to wrestle me to the ground. I hear the handcuffs click as they slap them onto my wrists.

So much for Independence Day. I guess I never really did get used to living with freedom.

* * *

42 **local** örtlich
43 **clerk** Verkäufer
44 **sweepstake** Gewinnspiel
53 **to deal** mit Drogen handeln
54 **stint** Zeit in einer Strafanstalt
54 **juvenile detention center** Jugendstrafanstalt
58 **to head for** auf etw. zugehen
60 **straightaway** sofort
62 **whaddya...?** what do you...?
66 **to stammer** stottern
66 **fixed** fixiert
67 **dumb** dumm
74 **to draw** ziehen
76 **to wrestle** ringen
77 **wrist** Handgelenk
78 **to get used to sth** sich an etw. gewöhnen

Independence Day: July 4th

The *Fourth of July* is probably the most important federal holiday in the United States. It commemorates the Declaration of Independence which was signed on July 4, 1776. For centuries beforehand, the U.S. was not a country in its own right, but a series of colonies. These thirteen colonies belonged to Great Britain. The
5 King of England was their head of state, British parliament made their laws, and their taxes were sent to London. As the American colonies became wealthier and less dependent on London for their survival, they wanted more power for themselves. By then, the European settlers saw themselves as Americans. They fought a war against their British colonial masters, receiving help from France,
10 Spain and the Netherlands who gave them ammunition and weapons. It was during the war that the Declaration of Independence was signed, but it wasn't until after the war, in 1783, when peace was officially made and the Declaration of Independence was recognized internationally, that the United States of America officially became a new and independent country. Today, Americans celebrate the
15 Fourth of July with parades, fireworks and barbecues. Most people put up American flags in their front yards. Ironically, most of the flags raised in the United States on the Fourth of July are imported from China.

2 **to commemorate** *gedenken*
2 **Declaration of Independence** *Unabhängigkeitserklärung*
3 **beforehand** *vorher*
5 **head of state** *Staatsoberhaupt*
6 **tax** *Steuer*
7 **dependent** *abhängig*
10 **ammunition** *Munition*
13 **recognized** *anerkannt*
15 **parade** *Umzug*
16 **front yard** *Vorgarten*

Locked up: The U.S. prison system

The United States has the world's largest prison population, making American
20 prisons a major social problem in what is still the richest country in the world. Almost 1 in every 100 adults is in prison or on parole. More Americans are in prison than the entire prison population of the largest 35 European countries together. Everyone agrees that the problem of U.S. prisons is getting worse, not better, and that something has to change. The number of inmates in U.S. prisons
25 tripled from the mid-1980s to 2010, although the rate of violent crime went down over the same period. The main reason for this development is the U.S. war on drugs. Over half of the inmates in U.S. prisons are there for drug-related crime, including possession of drugs and dealing. Most of these men and women are African-American or Hispanic and come from the poorer communities of the
30 United States. The increase in the number of people being sent to prison has, however, done little to help solve the U.S. drug problem. Moreover, the costs of keeping people in prison are high and the process of rehabilitating ex-prisoners into society is not working. Of every ten prisoners released, four will be back in prison within three years. This figure seriously questions the effectiveness of the
35 U.S. prison system in fighting crime.

21 **parole** *Bewährung*
24 **inmate** *Insasse*
25 **to triple** *verdreifachen*
25 **violent crime** *Gewaltdelikt*
28 **possession** *Besitz*
30 **increase** *Zunahme*
31 **to solve** *lösen*
33 **to release** *entlassen*
34 **figure** *Zahl*

Ziel: *Awareness*, Nachdenken über „Freiheit"
Aufgabe 1: Die SuS erstellen eine persönliche Liste von Freiheiten, die sie im Gefängnis nicht hätten und vergleichen sie anschließend mit der ihres Nachbarn.

pre-reading
KV 7.1, Aufg. 1
ca. 5 min.

Ziel: Textverständnis, Detailverständnis
Aufgaben 2 und 3: Im Anschluss lesen / hören die SuS den Text und tragen die Informationen, die sie dem Text entnehmen, ein. Partnerarbeit ist möglich. Anschließend werden die Lösungen im Klassenverband besprochen.

while-reading
KV 7.1, Aufg. 2, 3
ca. 15–20 min.

Ziel: vertieftes Textverständnis, Analyse des Ich-Erzählers
Aufgabe 4: Vor dem Bearbeiten der Aufgabe 4 sollte sichergestellt werden, dass der Begriff *irony* wirklich verstanden wird. Nach der Methode *Think-Pair-Share* bearbeiten die SuS die Aufgabe 4 erst in Einzelarbeit, vergleichen danach ihre Ergebnisse mit dem Partner und dann mit einem weiteren Paar. Die Gruppen werden aufgefordert, ihre Ergebnisse kurz im Plenum vorzustellen.
Nach der Ergebnissicherung könnte sich ein Vergleich zwischen den eigenen Freiheiten (Aufgabe 1) und den Bedürfnissen des Ich-Erzählers (Aufgabe 4a) anschließen.
Aufgabe 4 e) eignet sich auch für eine abschließende Diskussion.

post-reading
KV 7.2, Aufg. 4
ca. 25 min.

Vorschläge für weiterführende Aufgaben:
Ziel: persönliche Auseinandersetzung mit der Problematik der Rehabilitation von
   jugendlichen Kriminellen

Your turn: What would you do?
Some convicts keep in contact with the world outside by finding a pen pal and writing letters regularly. Imagine the first-person narrator was your pen pal.
– What would you tell him about the world outside prison to show him it might be worthwhile trying to live in it?
– How could he live a life outside the prison walls? What would he have to do to face and handle a life in freedom?

Write him a letter in which you give him hope and advice for the future.

Diese Aufgabe kann als Partneraufgabe oder als Hausaufgabe bearbeitet werden.

Mögliches Weiterarbeiten für stärkere Kurse: Weiterführung der Geschichte
   Two years later the first-person narrator appears on TV as a guest in a talk show titled "How I changed my life." The talk show host asks him what he is doing now and how he has managed to change his life for the better. Act it out!

1. Understanding the meaning of freedom

Before you read the story *Freedom* make a list of six things you would not have or could not do if you were in prison.

1. _____   4. _____

2. _____   5. _____

3. _____   6. _____

2. Background information:

Read the story. Fill in the information you get on the first-person narrator.

age: _____ place of residence: _____		criminal record:
family background: _____ _____ _____	education: _____ _____ _____	_____ _____ _____ _____

3. Understanding the story

a) This is a drawing of the scene of the first armed robbery. *Find seven mistakes.*

© Ernst Klett Sprachen GmbH, Stuttgart 2014 | www.klett.de | Alle Rechte vorbehalten
Kopieren für den eigenen Unterrichtsgebrauch gestattet.
ISBN 978-3-12-577343-X

3. **Understanding the story**

b) *Why were the boys caught so easily? Read lines 40–45 again and find three mistakes they made.*

1. _____

2. _____

3. _____

4. **Understanding the first-person narrator**

a) *Make a list of six things the first-person narrator has got or can do because he is back in prison.*

1. _____   4. _____

2. _____   5. _____

3. _____   6. _____

b) *Explain, why he committed the second robbery.*

_____

_____

_____

c) *Explain, why he went back to prison.*

_____

_____

_____

d) *Explain the sentence "I can't help seeing the irony of it." (l. 10)*

_____

_____

_____

e) *The first-person narrator is clearly a criminal. Is he also a bad person? Why (not)?*

_____

_____

_____

Patriot by David Fermer

"We are gathered here today to remember the men and women who died on September 11th, 2001." Mr. Lindford looked solemnly into the sea of faces below him. The entire school was gathered in the auditorium to commemorate Patriot Day.

5 "It is precisely 8:45," Mr. Lindford announced after glancing at his watch. "In exactly fifty-five seconds we will begin a minute's silence. 8:46 was the moment when the first American Airlines plane crashed into the North Tower of the World Trade Center. For that minute, the whole of America will be silent. I want you all to think about the men and women who died that day and say a prayer for them."

10 Mr. Lindford looked down to a girl in the front row. She was sitting with her head bowed, her elbows resting on her knees, looking at the floor. Her long black hair covered her face like a veil.

"In particular I want us to remember Carmen Rodriguez's father, one of the many who died in the Twin Towers that day," Lindford continued. "Mr. Rodriguez 15 was a hero. And that's what Patriot Day is all about: the heroes who make this country great."

Mr. Lindford waited for Carmen to look up, but she didn't. He cleared his throat awkwardly and looked at his watch again. "Ten seconds," he said and paused, counting slowly to himself. Then: "Let us begin…"

20 Silence filled the room. Outside the wind rocked the leaves on the trees. A bird cried. Somewhere, far away, a car sped past. Otherwise there was not a sound to be heard.

As she listened to the silence, Carmen closed her eyes and thought of her father. She had never really known him. She was only a few years old when he 25 died. Her mother used to tell her about him, who he was, where he came from, and what he liked. Carmen grew up in Queens, the daughter of a hero. Now she knew he wasn't a hero at all. Not since she had discovered his diaries.

Her mother had kept them in a box in the cellar, and Carmen had stumbled across them when they were packing to move to Angelo's. Angelo was Mom's 30 new "boyfriend". They'd been dating for years. Now Carmen's mom wanted to move in with him.

The diaries were beautifully bound books with black covers, six in total. Her father had written the period each book spanned on the front cover in silver ink. They traced the ten years before his death, starting with his arrival in the United 35 States and ending just before 9/11. Carmen asked her mother if she could read them. Her mother agreed.

So now Carmen knew Mr. Lindford was wrong. He had no idea. Her father wasn't a patriot. He wasn't a hero. He was a liar and a traitor. He hated this country, hated the United States government, wanted to make America hurt as 40 he had been hurting since arriving here. America, he wrote in his diary, made him

---

1 **to gather** *versammeln*
2 **solemnly** *ernst*
3 **auditorium** *Halle*
3 **to commemorate** *gedenken*
5 **to glance** *blicken*
6 **minute's silence** *Schweigeminute*
9 **prayer** *Gebet*
10 **row** *Reihe*
11 **bowed** *gebeugt*
12 **veil** *Schleier*
17 **to clear one's throat** *sich räuspern*
18 **awkwardly** *verlegen*
20 **leaf** *Blatt*
21 **to speed past** *vorbeirasen*
27 **diary** *Tagebuch*
28 **to stumble across sth** *auf etw. stoßen*
31 **to move in** *einziehen*
32 **bound** *gebunden*
33 **to span** *umfassen*
33 **ink** *Tinte*
34 **to trace** *beschreiben*
37 **liar** *Lügner*
37 **traitor** *Verräter*
39 **to hurt** *leiden*

feel like a second-class citizen. He and Carmen's mother were from the Dominican Republic. They came to the U.S. legally. They were poor. Carmen's father worked as a janitor at the World Trade Center. He found the work degrading, wanted something better, but couldn't find anything. Then he started to blame other
45 people. *This country is racist*, he wrote in his diary. *Anyone who is not white is automatically disadvantaged.* Elsewhere he wrote pages and pages about the power of money and capitalism. *In this country, only money counts. If you have no money, you are nobody.*

Carmen found it difficult to share her father's opinion. She had never
50 experienced racism herself. Her mother worked in a supermarket and was a low earner, but Carmen had never felt poor. What really shocked her most about her father's diaries was the anger behind his words. *What the British were to the 19th century, the Americans are today: economic colonists. Their only aim is to exploit weaker nations and fill their own pockets. Someone should teach this country a*
55 *lesson. They should hit America where it hurts, take it off its high horse. If I could find a way to make America open its eyes, I would. I would shake some sense into this country.*

This wasn't the voice of a hero. These opinions could never be shared by a true patriot. For years Carmen had come to see her father as the man everyone told
60 her he was. Suddenly that image was shattered.

Carmen told her mother about what she'd read in her father's diaries, and soon another truth emerged: Carmen's parents were about to separate before that tragic day in September. Carmen's father had become unbearable. Her mother couldn't live with him anymore. He was paranoid, sick. He blamed
65 everyone else for his situation. He blamed Carmen's mother, he blamed the U.S. government, he blamed the history of the Dominican Republic.

"There was something very wrong with your father," her mother told her. "I tried to help him, but I couldn't. He refused to see a doctor."

The minute's silence came to an end. "Thank you." A few people coughed. Mr.
70 Lindford looked at Carmen. Carmen looked up.

"Would you like to say a word?" Lindford asked.

Carmen slowly got to her feet. As she stepped onto the stage, she could feel all eyes upon her. In front of the microphone she took a moment to focus, clearing her throat. Then she began to speak. "Hello," she said meekly. "Um… I just wanted
75 to say… thank you. Thank you for your thoughts, for your prayers. And thank you, Mr. Lindford, for your kind words about my father… Yes, my father was a hero. A real hero. He was a patriot who loved America. And I love America, too."

* * *

41 second-class citizen *Bürger zweiter Klasse*
43 janitor *Reinigungskraft*
43 degrading *erniedrigend*
44 to blame sb *jdm die Schuld geben*
49 to share an opinion *eine Meinung teilen*
50 low earner *Geringverdiener*
53 to exploit *ausbeuten*
54 to teach sb a lesson *jdm eine Lektion erteilen*
60 shattered *zerbrochen*
62 to emerge *herauskommen*
62 to separate *sich trennen*
63 unbearable *unerträglich*
68 to refuse *sich weigern*
69 to cough *husten*
73 to focus *sich konzentrieren*
74 meekly *sanftmütig*

Patriot Day: September 11ᵗʰ

Although Patriot Day is not a federal holiday across the country, it is an important remembrance day in the United States. It takes place every year on September 11ᵗʰ and is dedicated to the people killed in the terrorist attacks which struck America on September 11ᵗʰ, 2001. These attacks changed the face of world
5 politics. They began at 08:46 a.m. Eastern time, when an American Airlines airplane from Boston crashed into the North Tower of New York City's World Trade Center, once the tallest building in the world and a symbol of American capitalism. Seventeen minutes later, another airplane crashed into the South Tower, while at 09:37 a.m. a third airplane crashed into the Pentagon, the headquarters of the
10 United States Department of Defense near Washington, D.C. 2,977 innocent people died in these attacks. The events marked the beginning of the U.S.-led "War on Terror". On Patriot Day the American flag is flown at half-staff as a sign of respect. There is a minute's silence at 8:46 a.m. Eastern time, the moment when the first plane crashed into the North Tower. Memorial services take place
15 throughout the country, in particular at the site of the attack in New York.

1 **across** *überall*
2 **to take place** *stattfinden*
3 **dedicated** *gewidmet*
4 **to strike** *treffen*
9 **headquarters** *Hauptquartier*
10 **Department of Defense** *Verteidigungsministerium*
10 **innocent** *unschuldig*
11 **U.S.-led** *angeführt von den USA*
12 **half-staff** *halbmast*
14 **service** *Gottesdienst*
15 **site** *Ort*

Buenos Días: The Hispanic community in the USA

More than 50 million people of Latin American descent live in the United States. They represent the largest ethnic minority in the country. Latin Americans are people who come from the Spanish and Portuguese-speaking countries of
20 Central and South America. They are often called Hispanics or Latinos. There are more Spanish speakers living in the USA than in Argentina, Colombia or even Spain! Only one other country in the world has more Spanish speakers than the USA and that is Mexico. People of Latino descent have been in the U.S. ever since the first Spanish colonists settled in Florida. Several of the southern states, like
25 Texas and New Mexico, once belonged to Mexico. Mexicans make up more than half of the Latinos living in the States, followed by Puerto Ricans and Cubans. It is estimated that in the year 2050 the Hispanic population of the United States will be more than 130 million people, making up over 30% of the population. Most Latinos in the USA were born there and most of them are U.S. citizens. Almost
30 half of the Latino population in the USA lives either in California or Texas. Many Hispanic families still speak Spanish at home, but most Hispanics who were born in the USA speak fluent English.

17 **descent** *Abstammung*
18 **minority** *Minderheit*
24 **several** *mehrere*
25 **to belong** *gehören*
27 **to estimate** *schätzen*
29 **citizen** *Bürger*
32 **fluent** *fließend*

Ziel: *Awareness,* Wortschatzarbeit

Aufgabe 1 a/b: Die SuS erarbeiten mit einem Partner Vorstellungen der Begriffe *racist, liar, hero* und *patriot,* damit ihnen diese in späteren Diskussionen zur Verfügung stehen. Die Lösungen werden im Klassenverband verglichen. Anschließend wird die Geschichte *Patriot* gemeinsam gehört / gelesen und Fragen zum Verständnis werden geklärt.

pre-reading
KV 8.1, Aufg. 1
ca. 10–15 min

Ziel: Sicherung des Textverständnisses, Hörverständnis

Die Geschichte wird ein- bis zweimal von CD vorgespielt, dabei bearbeiten die SuS Aufgabe 2. Die Lösungen können im Klassenverband oder mithilfe einer vorbereiteten Folie schnell verglichen werden.

while-reading
KV 8.1, Aufg. 2
ca. 10 min

Ziel: Sicherung des Textverständnis, einem Text Informationen entnehmen

Die SuS lesen die Geschichte und tragen die Informationen in die vorgegebenen Spalten (*keywords only*) ein. Sie arbeiten dabei in Einzel- oder Partnerarbeit. Die Überprüfung erfolgt im Klassenverband.

KV 8.1, Aufg. 3
ca. 5–10 min.

Ziel: vertieftes Textverständnis; Auseinandersetzung mit dem Thema „Patriotismus", creative writing

Die **Aufgabe 4a)** knüpft an die Aufgabe 1 an. Die SuS erarbeiten sich in Diskussionen nach der *Think! Pair! Share!* Methode eine Einschätzung von Carmens Motivation, ihren Vater wider besseren Wissens als patriotischen Helden darzustellen. Dabei ist es möglich, dass hier zwei unterschiedliche Gewichtungen aufeinander treffen: Carmen lügt, da sie selbst nicht als Tochter eines Verräters dastehen möchte versus Carmen liebt Amerika und möchte dem Anlass *Patriot Day* gerecht werden, d. h. sie handelt aus patriotischen Gesichtspunkten. Diese Diskussion soll am Text geführt werden (z. B. unter Bezug auf den Titel der Geschichte) und wird in der Hausaufgabe Aufgabe 4 d) noch einmal explizit aufgegriffen.

post-reading
KV 8.2, Aufg. 4
ca. 60 min.

Die **Aufgaben 4 b)** und **c)** nähern sich der gleichen Thematik unter einem anderen Gesichtspunkt: *Was wäre passiert, hätte Carmen die Wahrheit über ihren Vater gesagt?* Das kreative Schreiben wird hier in zwei Schritten und in Partnerarbeit organisiert. Auf diese Weise werden alle Beiträge gewürdigt, da mindestens ein Partner auf den Beitrag reagiert.

Schritt 1: Die SuS haben 20 Minuten Zeit, um Carmens alternative Rede zu schreiben. Die SuS sollen dabei auf ein freies Blatt Papier schreiben, so dass genug Platz vorhanden ist, damit der Partner die Geschichte auf demselben Blatt (unter der Rede) fortsetzen kann.

> **Tipp** *Bus-Stop-Methode:* Wer fertig ist, stellt sich mit seinem Papier an eine imaginäre Bushaltestelle und wartet, bis der nächste Schüler fertig ist. Dieser wird sein Partner.

Schritt 2: Die SuS tauschen die Reden, lesen die Rede ihres Partners und setzen die Geschichte mit der Reaktion des Publikums auf diese Rede fort. (Zeitrahmen 20 Min.)

Schritt 3: Einzelne Paare lesen ihre Geschichten der Klasse vor. (20 Min.)

Ziel: Eigenständige, weiterführende Arbeit zum Thema 9/11, Internetrecherche

Differenzierung für stärkere Lerngruppen: Die Aufgabe 5 kann als weiterführende Hausaufgabe oder als weiterführende Projektarbeit behandelt werden.

KV 8.2, Aufg. 5

Internetzugang nötig!

1. Before you read the story: Terminology

Work with a partner.

a) Explain the following words in one or two sentences: "racist", "liar". Start like this:

A racist is a person who _____

A liar is _____

b) Describe a situation that exemplifies[1] the two following terms: "hero", "patriot".

a hero:	**a patriot:**

2. Close reading: *Right, wrong* or *not in the text?*

Tick the right answer. Correct the wrong sentences.

	right	wrong	not in the text
1. Carmen's father died in the attack on the Twin Towers.			
2. Carmen's parents are illegal immigrants.			
3. Carmen's father beat her mother.			
4. Carmen's mother married again.			
5. Carmen read her father's diaries.			
6. There were ten diaries.			
7. Carmen is good at school.			
8. Carmen is proud of her father.			
9. Carmen's father went to the doctor because he was mentally ill.			

3. Carmen and her family

Work with a partner. Take notes on what you know about them.

	Carmen's father	Carmen's mother	Carmen
Where did / do they come from? Where did they grow up?			
What was / is their job?			
What did / do they think of America and the Americans?			
What did / do they think of their life in America?			

---

[1] **to exemplify** veranschaulichen, als Beispiel dienen für

4. **On Patriot Day**

   a) *Think – Pair – Share:*

   Why doesn't Carmen tell the audience the truth about her father on Patriot Day?
   Give reasons, why you think so.

   _____

   _____

   b) *A new ending – part 1:*

   What would happen, if she told the audience about what she had found out about her father? What would she say to the audience?

   Complete her speech (about five to eight sentences) on a separate piece of paper. It starts like this:

   Carmen slowly got to her feet. As she stepped onto the stage, she could feel all eyes upon her. In front of the microphone she took a moment to focus, clearing her throat. Then she began to speak. "Hello," she said meekly. "Um… I just wanted to say …

   c) *A new ending – part 2:*

   How would the audience react? What would her friends say? What would the teachers say and do?

   Find a partner, exchange your speeches from task 4 b). Read your partner's speech and underneath write down in five to eight sentences how the audience might react.

   d) *Homework:*

   Choose one of the questions and say what you think. Give reasons why you think so. Write about eight to ten sentences.

   Is Carmen a liar?   *OR*   **Is Carmen a patriot?**

5. **How did 9/11 affect the people?**

   a) *Ask five adults where they were and what they did on 9/11. You will probably hear five very personal stories. Discuss and take notes: why do people all over the world remember that day?*

   _____

   _____

   b) *Gallery 9/11*

   The two following websites provide lots of information, pictures and personal stories of survivors and families affected by 9/11. Many of them are informative, many of them are emotional. Browse the different categories, look at the pictures. Then choose one that you find most interesting or touching, copy it or print it out and inform your classmates what it is about.

   - *http://11-sept.org/home.html*
   - *http://www.huffingtonpost.com/2012/09/11/9-11-survivors-_n_1872278.html*

Indian Elvis by David Fermer

You sometimes do crazy things when you're young. You don't think about what will happen if things go wrong, about the consequences. You think there's nothing you can't do, nothing you can't handle. Being young is good and bad at the same time. You do things just for the hell of it. You live for the moment. But
5 sometimes there's a heavy price to pay for not thinking ahead.

When I was seventeen, I did a crazy thing, and the price I paid was more than I'd ever imagined. To understand my story, you have to understand America. I'm a Native American, what people used to call an "Indian". They've changed that name now, no one calls us "Indians" anymore, but we're still the same people. The Native
10 Americans were the people that lived in this country before the white man came. The Europeans. Bit by bit they took our land and very nearly killed us off. Then, much later, they got a guilty conscience and tried to make it up to us, without giving us our land back or leaving our country, because by then it was their country. So they put us on "reservations". Indian reservations. Land which was of
15 no interest to them, because there were no minerals on it, no oil, no water mostly, nothing they wanted. These reservations became our home. We call them "rez" for short. I grew up on a rez in Arizona. That's where my people come from. I belong to the Navajo tribe. And the Navajo, like many other Native American people, like to celebrate life. Once a year, the whole tribe gets together and there
20 is dancing and singing and eating and drinking and everyone has a good time and feels proud about where they come from and who they are. We call these celebrations "powwows". You would call them a party.

I turned seventeen at the end of the 1950s. That's a long time ago. Back then, Native Americans were second-class citizens. Actually, we were third-class citizens.
25 The African-Americans had the pleasure of being second-class citizens. Neither group had equal rights. The white man was boss, and he wanted it to stay that way. So we Native Americans, the true inheritors of this country, stayed on our reservations and kept to ourselves.

Only occasionally did we leave our land. Our fathers often worked outside the
30 rez, on building sites, doing manual labor. Every now and again, our mothers left the rez to go shopping in the city. Flagstaff was our closest town. One day, just before our annual powwow, my mother sent me into town to buy provisions. After I had done the rounds, I saw a special offer being advertised at the local cinema: a matinee ticket for only 10 cents. It was so cheap, I couldn't say no. So
35 before I left town, I bought myself a ticket, went into the auditorium, and watched a film called "Jailhouse Rock" with a guy who looked just like me, singing and dancing like I had never seen anyone sing and dance before. His name was Elvis and he was mind-blowing!

3 **to handle** *fertig werden mit*
4 **just for the hell of it** *zum Spaß*
5 **to think ahead** *voraus-denken*
11 **to kill off** *ausrotten*
12 **guilty conscience** *schlechtes Gewissen*
12 **to make up** *sich versöhnen*
24 **second-class citizen** *Bürger zweiter Klasse*
26 **equal rights** *gleiche Rechte*
27 **inheritor** *Erbe*
29 **occasionally** *gelegentlich*
30 **manual labor** *körperliche Arbeit*
32 **annual** *jährlich*
32 **provisions** *Vorräte*
33 **to do the rounds** *die Runde machen*
33 **special offer** *Sonderangebot*
38 **mind-blowing** *irre gut*

So when I got back to the rez, I went straight to the powwow committee and
40 put my name down for the dancing competition. The dancing competition is the
most important part of any powwow. We Native Americans are great dancers. We
have many different styles. All our dances mean something. They tell a story. They
pass on a message. They are prayers to the spirits around us. Drummers drum.
People sing. Dancers dance.

45 By the time the powwow started a week later, I had rehearsed my performance
to perfection. I remember waiting for my turn in the main tent, watching the
other dancers. They were all wearing traditional clothes, long robes, elaborate
headdresses, their faces painted. I was wearing tight black pants. My shirt was
unbuttoned, open to my chest. My thick black hair was gelled back with pomade.
50 I was Elvis. The King of Rock 'n' Roll.

When it was my turn, I stepped out onto the dance floor and the whole tent
fell silent. I had already told the drummers I didn't need any music, that I would
be singing myself. So before the silence made me have second thoughts, I started.
"One, two, … one, two, three…" – my hands clapping, the contrabass setting the
55 beat in my head, the trumpets, the snare drums. I didn't dance for the moon or
the sun. I danced for me.

At first my people watched me in silence, speechless, but soon their surprise
gave way to anger as the elders began to shout. Be silent! Shame on you! This is
the music of the white man! I continued to sing and dance, hoping the music
60 would infect them as it had infected me, but when the first beer cans started
flying into my face, followed by half-eaten fruit and bread, I left the stage.

My father beat me that same night. He said I had brought shame on his family.
I told him that Elvis had Cherokee blood, but that only made him beat me more.
My dance was an insult to our people. The U.S. government had just discovered
65 uranium on our land. They had given several mining companies permission to
start mining. It was the same story all over again: my people were left to go
hungry while the white man got rich. And I was dancing to his music!

I left the rez the next day. I turned my back on my people, left their world and
became part of the other America, the America of infinite possibilities. Over the
70 next few years I became famous all over the country. From Los Angeles to New
York, from Chicago to Tennessee. They called me the "Indian Elvis". I had a great
life, but I never stopped missing my people.

And now I've come back because I'm dying. I want to die among my own
people. Soon my body will move on to the spirit world, and I will become a part
75 of everything around me. This is what my people believe. And, who knows, maybe
after I die, I will meet the real Elvis, the King of Rock 'n' Roll, and then – finally –
we can sing and dance together.

* * *

43 **to pass on** *weitergeben*
43 **prayer** *Gebet*
43 **spirit** *Geist*
45 **performance** *Auftritt*
48 **headdress** *Kopfschmuck*
49 **unbuttoned** *aufgeknöpft*
49 **chest** *Brust*
49 **gelled** *gegelt*
53 **to have second thoughts**
  es sich anders überlegen
57 **speechless** *sprachlos*
58 **elder** *Ältere(r)*
58 **shame on you!** *schäm dich!*
60 **to infect** *anstecken*
62 **to beat** *schlagen*
62 **shame** *Schande*
64 **insult** *Beleidigung*
65 **uranium** *Uran*
65 **mining** *Bergbau*
65 **permission** *Genehmigung*
69 **infinite** *unendlich*
69 **possibility** *Möglichkeit*

The Native American Powwow

Today, Native Americans in the USA and Canada are proud of their cultural heritage. After centuries of oppression, and due to a growing awareness about the way Native Americans were mistreated by previous U.S. governments, Native American tribes celebrate their cultural heritage in a gathering known as a
5 "powwow". The word *powwow* comes from an old American Indian word for "spiritual leader", and in many ways the powwow is a spiritual celebration. In the time before the Europeans colonized North America, there were many different Native American cultures living throughout the continent. Just as Italians, Germans and Hungarians are culturally different in Europe, so too were the
10 Native Americans diverse in ethnicity and culture. There were, however, similarities. Most Native American tribes didn't worship gods or one God like the Europeans. Their belief system was rooted in nature and a spirit world in which all living things – from animals to trees, to thunder and lightning – had a spirit. Many tribes believed they were created from the earth itself, from the waters or the
15 stars. At the annual powwows, the Native American nations celebrate this belief system. A grand opening ceremony starts the powwow, which often lasts for up to one week, followed by dancing competitions and music performances, where drums play an important role in communicating between the human, animal and spirit world.

2 **heritage** *Erbe*
2 **oppression** *Unterdrückung*
2 **awareness** *Bewusstsein*
3 **to mistreat** *misshandeln*
3 **previous** *vorig*
4 **gathering** *Zusammenkunft*
10 **diverse** *vielfältig*
11 **to worship** *anbeten*
12 **rooted** *verwurzelt*
15 **annual** *jährlich*
16 **to last** *andauern*

A short history of Native American life in the USA

Almost three million Native Americans are still living in the USA today. It is estimated that anywhere between 40 and 100 million people lived on the North American continent, from Mexico to Canada, before the first Europeans arrived. This catastrophic decline in numbers is the result of a complex series of causes.
25 After Christopher Columbus discovered the New World in 1492, European immigration to America began slowly. The first immigrants were not antagonistic to the Native American population. They tried to understand the native culture, learn from their hunting and farming methods, and live side by side. But they also brought diseases with them that were unknown to the North American natives.
30 As the North American colonies grew and the U.S. declared independence in 1776, it soon became clear that America could no longer support parallel cultures. The "new" Americans wanted to develop their country and make it their own, and their expansion from east to west became increasingly aggressive and systematic, especially in their dealings with Native Americans. By the end of the 19th century,
35 most Native American tribes had either been wiped out or were forced to live on reservations where they were often isolated and left to go hungry on land that was seldom suitable for farming or hunting.

22 **to estimate** *schätzen*
24 **decline** *Rückgang*
24 **cause** *Ursache*
27 **population** *Bevölkerung*
28 **hunting** *Jagen*
29 **disease** *Krankheit*
31 **to support** *unterstützen*
33 **expansion** *Ausbreitung*
33 **increasingly** *zunehmend*
34 **dealings with** *Umgang mit*
35 **to wipe out** *auslöschen*
37 **suitable** *geeignet*

Ziel: *Awareness*, Nachdenken über *cultural identity*

Aufgabe 1: Die SuS stellen anhand der von ihnen gewählten Begriffe ihre eigene kulturelle Identität der Kleingruppe vor. Anschließend wird die Geschichte *Indian Elvis* gemeinsam gehört / gelesen und Fragen zum Verständnis werden geklärt.

Tipp: Da nicht allen SuS Elvis Presley bekannt sein dürfte, bietet es sich an, Fotos und einen Song vorbereitet zu haben, um einen Eindruck des Künstlers zu vermitteln. Es kann ein Ausschnitt aus dem Film *Jailhouse Rock* gezeigt werden, z. B. http://www.youtube.com/watch?v=qDID_E0FDUU.

pre-reading
KV 9.1, Aufg. 1
ca. 15 min.

Ziel: vertieftes Textverständnis, der Aspekt der *cultural identity*; freies Sprechen

Die SuS bekommen ca. 25 Minuten Zeit, um die Aufgaben 2 a)–d) vorzubereiten. Anschließend schlüpft ein Gruppenmitglied in die Rolle des Ich-Erzählers und trägt das Gruppenergebnis aus dessen Sicht vor. Die anderen Schüler dürfen auch Fragen stellen *(Hot Seat)*.

post-reading
KV 9.1, Aufg. 2
ca. 45 min.
Hot Seat,

Hieran schließt sich eine allgemeine Klassendiskussion um den Begriff der *cultural identity* an, bei der die SuS auch Gelegenheit haben sollten, zu ihrer eigenen kulturellen Identität und ggf. zum Leben zwischen zwei Kulturen Stellung zu nehmen.

KV 9.1, Aufg. 3
ca. 15 min.

Ziele: Aktivierung von Vorwissen zur Geschichte der *Native Americans*

Aufgabe 1: Die SuS tragen in Partnerarbeit ihr Vorwissen bzw. auch ihre Vorurteile über die Kultur und Geschichte der Ureinwohner Amerikas zusammen. Dabei dürfen gern Hinweise auf die *Pilgrim Fathers* und das erste *Thanksgiving*, ev. *Pocahontas* oder die Schlacht am *Wounded Knee* gegeben werden.

In Aufgabe 1 b) hinterfragen die SuS ihr Vorwissen kritisch.

Mögliche Differenzierung für stärkere Kurse: Aufgabe 1 c) als Hausaufgabe

KV 9.2, Aufg. 1
ca. 15 min.

Ziel: vertieftes Textverständnis; Auseinandersetzung mit dem Thema „Umgehen mit Angehörigen indigener Völker damals und heute"

Die SuS arbeiten arbeitsteilig in Gruppen. Sie entscheiden sich für eines der beiden Themen, nachdem sie die Kurzbeschreibung gelesen haben. Dabei muss sichergestellt werden, dass beide Themen / Artikel bearbeitet werden. Bevor sich die SuS gemeinsam ihren Artikel erschließen, erstellen sie eigene Kriterien für „faires" Verhalten bzw. antizipieren Probleme von Teenagern in einem Reservat. Im Anschluss überprüfen sie die Praxis anhand des Artikels vor dem Hintergrund ihrer eigenen, vorher entwickelten Vorstellungen / Werte und präsentieren ihre Ergebnisse der Klasse. Da die einzelnen Gruppen vermutlich verschiedene Ideen entwickeln, bietet sich eine anschließende Diskussion darüber an, wie sie ihre Vorstellungen begründen, inwieweit sie haltbar sind, inwiefern die Realität mit ihren Vorstellungen übereinstimmt oder abweicht.

KV 9.2, Aufg. 2
ca. 45 min. + 30 min.
Internetzugang nötig!
Alternativ: Ausdrucke der Texte der angegebenen Webseiten

1. **Before you read the story:** Work in groups of three or four.
   a) *Think of three things that you consider important for your cultural identity. They can be objects (e.g. certain foods) or abstract things like music or paintings. Write them into the speech bubbles.*

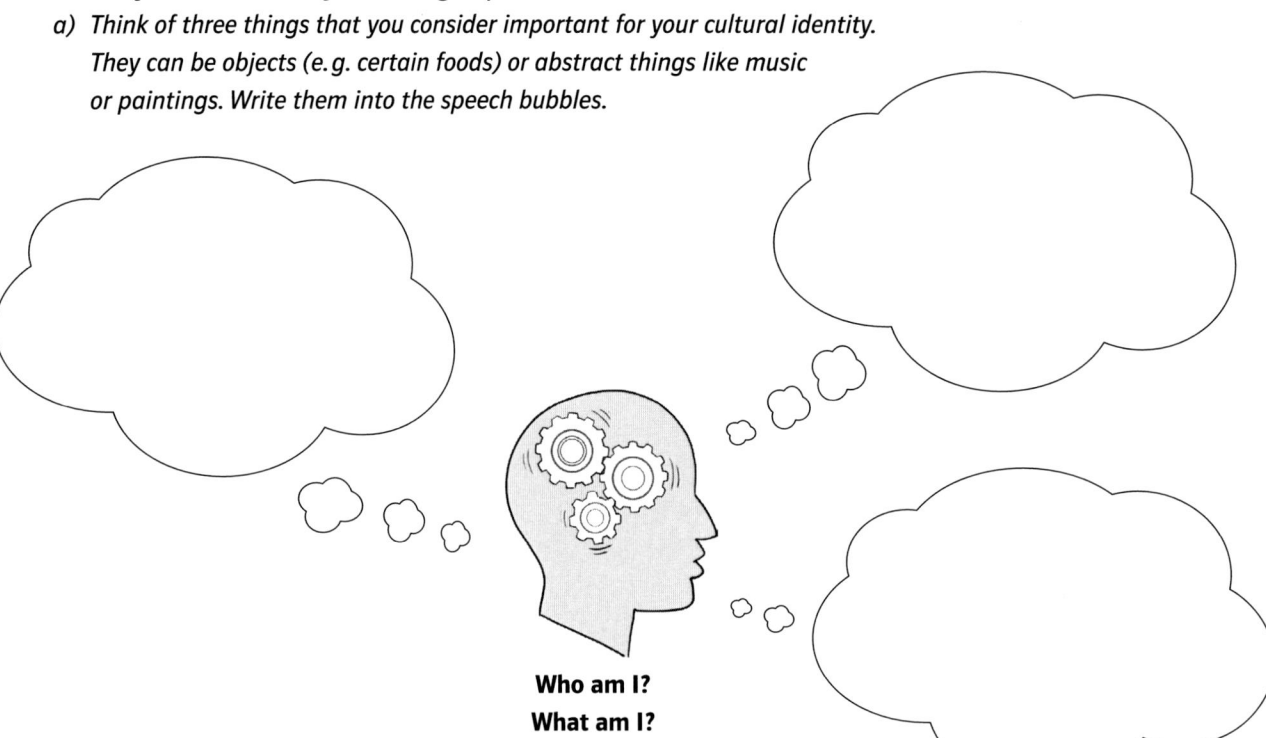

Who am I?
What am I?

   b) *Introduce these things to your group. Explain, what they mean to you and your personal cultural identity. How do you see yourself?*

2. **After you have read the story:** Get into groups of 3–4 students and work through tasks a)–d).
   a) *If the "Indian Elvis" were given task 1 above – which three things might he choose? What would he say about them? How would he describe his cultural identity?*

   b) *Find hints in the text which can support your choices.*

   c) *Choose one member of your group who will represent the "Indian Elvis" and who will explain your group's choices to your class. The class can also ask him / her questions ("Hot Seat").*

   d) *Find proof in the text that the first-person narrator regrets having left his people and having given up his Navajo identity.*

3. **Discussion:**
   Discuss the following aspects of "cultural identity" and take notes on the results of your discussion:
   • What contributes to *cultural identity*?
   • How important are birthplace, parents, upbringing, school, media, religion, music, food etc. for your cultural identity?
   • Can your cultural identity change?
   • How might other people (e.g. your family) react if you changed your cultural identity?

4. **Homework:**
   Consider the results of your discussion. Write a text about your own cultural identity with reference to the questions you talked about.

Native Americans *vs*. White European settlers

1. **What do you already know about the history of Native American people? Work with a partner.**

    a) *Make a mind map in which you collect anything you may have heard, read or seen about Native Americans.*

    b) *What are your sources? Where do your ideas about Native Americans come from?*

    c) ***Optional:*** *Look at your mind map. Which of your ideas may not be true? Choose one or two points and verify or falsify them by using sources like history books, the Internet, articles etc.*

2. **Unfair past – fair present? Work in groups of three to four.**

    Nobody will dispute that the white European settlers treated the Native Americans very unfairly in the past. This story only mentions little of the unjust and inhumane treatment Native Americans had to suffer since the arrival of the "white man".

    a) *Look at the story and make a list of all the injustices and indignities Native Americans had to suffer at the hands of the white European settlers.*

What was done to the Native Americans?	Line(s) in the text

    b) *But what is the situation of Native Americans like today? Do they still live on reservations? Do they have a good life there? Are they still being treated unfairly by the whites?*

Choose one of the following two aspects of life on a reservation:

Oil / Gas drilling on reservations	The lives of young Native Americans
http://www.nytimes.com/2012/08/16/us/montana-tribe-divided-on-tapping-oil-rich-land.html?	http://www.washingtonpost.com/world/national-security/the-hard-lives--and-high-suicide-rate--of-native-american-children/2014/03/09/6e0ad9b2-9f03-11e3-b8d8-94577ff66b28_story.html
Collectively, the reservations contain about 3% of the United States' oil and gas deposits, or 25 billion cubic feet of as-of-yet undeveloped natural gas reserves. *Discuss in your group, what you would consider fair treatment of the Native Americans on whose reservation the natural resources were found.*	There is growing alarm about the number of young Native Americans taking their own lives – more than three times the national average, and up to 10 times on some reservations. *Discuss in your group what could be the biggest problems of Native American teenagers living on a reservation.*
Now read the article and find out about the advantages and disadvantages of exploiting the natural resources on reservations. *Take notes.*	Now read the article and find out about living conditions and problems of teenage Native Americans. *Take notes.*

13th Street by David Fermer

Everyone knows the number 13 is unlucky, but does anyone know why? I mean, it's just a number! People always say bad things happen on Friday 13th, but they never do. At least, no more than any other day. Just because some Italian composer called Rossini died on Friday 13th ages ago... Big deal! That doesn't mean we're
5 all going to die on Friday 13th. Plus there were thirteen people at the Last Supper, so I guess that was a bad day for Jesus.

Did you know that most skyscrapers in Downtown Detroit don't have a 13th floor? The elevator can take you from the 1st to the 20th story except for the 13th, because there isn't one. That's superstition for you!

10 So when my friends and I got together to go out this year on Halloween, Mom told me under no circumstances were we to go anywhere near 13th Street.

"Why, Mom? It's just a street!"

"No, it's not. It's a *deserted* street, and we all know what happens to deserted streets in this city."

15 Yeah, the drug addicts move in and make it their home, and you can smell the streets from miles away because they are so out of it, they forget to wash or brush their teeth and so they just rot away.

"Okay, Mom. Promise!"

Needless to say, we're not going trick-or-treating. That's just what we told my
20 parents. They think it's really cute that a group of 15-year-olds still wants to dress up and go from door to door asking for candy, but the truth is, we're going to a party. I have a really cool costume this year. It's this amazing green dress with all these sequins. A cross between Twilight, Avatar and Star Wars. I look so hot.

We meet at my place and get dressed. Greg is Frankenstein, Madison is a
25 witch, Aidan is going as a skeleton. It takes us a while to get ready, but when we're finished, we look in the mirror and laugh.

Dad wishes us good luck as we leave and reminds me not to go to 13th Street, and the four of us all say "Yes, Mr. Kirby!" (except I say "Yes, Dad!") at the same time, and then we leave.

30 The way to the party takes us past 13th Street. We stop and look down the street. There are no lights on anywhere. The houses are all boarded up. The wind whistles down the alleyways. A trash can falls over at the other end of the street and rolls over the ground.

"I dare you to go in," I say to Aidan.

35 "*You* go in!" says Aidan.

"We can all go in," I suggest.

"But your dad said..." Madison doesn't finish her sentence.

"Let's do it," says Greg, stepping into the street.

The four of us enter 13th street. It's so quiet that the only thing I can hear is
40 Greg breathing and the sound of Madison's heels on the asphalt. The wind blows some trash across the street. Empty bottles rattle. Greg stops in front of the house with no roof. "Look! There's a light on!"

3 **at least** *jedenfalls*
3 **composer** *Komponist*
4 **big deal!** *na und!*
5 **the Last Supper** *das letzte Abendmahl*
8 **except** *außer*
9 **superstition** *Aberglaube*
11 **under no circumstances** *keinesfalls*
13 **deserted** *verlassen*
15 **drug addict** *Drogen-abhängige(r)*
17 **to rot** *verroten*
19 **needless to say** *selbstverständlich*
20 **cute** *süß*
20 **to dress up** *sich verkleiden*
21 **candy** *Süßigkeiten*
23 **sequin** *Paillette*
23 **a cross** *eine Mischung*
31 **to board up** *mit Brettern zunageln*
32 **alleyway** *Gasse*
32 **trash can** *Mülltonne*
34 **to dare sb to do sth** *jdn herausfordern, etw. zu tun*
40 **heels** *Absätze*
41 **to rattle** *klappern*

On the ground floor, behind the boarded windows, a light is flickering.

"What now?" I ask.

45   "We do what you told your parents," Greg smiles. "Trick or treat!"

He goes up to the broken steps and knocks on the door. Aidan laughs nervously and says, "You're crazy!" No one answers. Greg knocks again. I go up the steps and try to pull him away. "Come on! Let's go." But before we can leave, the door opens.

"What d'you want?" The guy standing in front of us looks like he's dressed up

50   for his own Halloween party, except he's for real. His face is as white as a sheet; he has black rings around his eyes, no teeth between his lips. His clothes are torn and dirty.

"Nothing!" says Greg, backing off. "We're just trick-or-treating."

"You got a treat for me?" asks the man. "Come on! Give me a treat!"

55   He holds out his hand and takes a step towards us, but we've already turned around and are running. "Sorry! Wrong address!"

We don't stop running until we're out of the street. We don't look back once. As soon as we're in safety, Aidan's the first to laugh. "You should have seen your face!" he says, pointing at Greg. "'*We're just trick-or-treating!*' You were terrified!"

60   "He looked like a zombie!" I say, laughing as well. Then Greg and Madison start laughing, too, and we can't stop, so nobody hears the man who comes up to us from behind until he says, "What's the big joke?"

We turn around and see him: a guy dressed as Death. Long black cloak, white mask, black eyes. A scythe in his hand.

65   "We just met this guy from 13th Street," explains Greg, still laughing. "He looked like a zombie."

"He did?" Death's voice is deep and colorless.

"Don't go in there," I joke with him. "That street is messed up."

"It would be," says Death. "It's 13th Street. And I live there."

70   Before I realize what's going on, the man raises his scythe and swings it down across Madison's face. Blood explodes from her eyes. I scream. Aidan and Greg start to run, but Death brings his scythe down on Aidan's back, taking him down. As Aidan falls lifeless to the ground, Death's mask slips off his face, and I see … it's my *dad*. I scream even louder, and suddenly I'm sitting in my bed and the door

75   flies open and Dad comes running into the room asking me what the hell the matter is and, as he takes me in his arms, I realize I was dreaming.

That's the last time I lie to my parents.

* * *

43 **to flicker** *flackern*
50 **sheet** *Laken*
51 **torn** *zerrissen*
59 **to be terrified** *große Angst haben*
63 **Death** *der Tod*
63 **cloak** *Umhang*
64 **scythe** *Sense*
68 **to joke** *scherzen*
68 **messed up** *hier: krank*
73 **to slip off** *herunterrutschen*
75 **what's the matter?** *was ist los?*
77 **to lie** *lügen*

Halloween: October 31st

Halloween is celebrated every year on October 31st, the night before All Saints Day on November 1st. It is also known as "All Hallows Eve" (*hallow* means "holy", and *eve* is an old English word for "evening"). Historians think that the festival originally started in Ireland and was called *Samhain*. This Celtic festival marked
5 the end of the summer. Bonfires were lit and the souls of the dead were said to revisit their homes. Later the Celtic pagan festival of Samhain mixed with the Christian festival of All Saints Day. All Saints Day wasn't just a time for honoring the saints, it was also a time for praying for the dead who were on their way to heaven. In the Middle Ages, beggars went from door to door on October 31st
10 praying for souls in return for food – a ritual which later became the basis for the trick-or-treating tradition. By the 17th century, Halloween was firmly established in Catholic Scotland and Ireland, and it was the Irish immigrants who brought the tradition to the USA in the 19th century. On Halloween, people typically get dressed up in costumes representing supernatural figures and children go trick-or-
15 treating, asking for candy or "threatening" a "trick" if they do not get any. Another tradition is to carve pumpkins into jack-o-lanterns.

1 **All Saints Day** Allerheiligen
5 **bonfire** Freudenfeuer
5 **to light** anzünden
6 **to revisit** einen Ort nochmals besuchen
6 **pagan** Ungläubiger
7 **to honor** ehren
8 **to pray** beten
9 **beggar** Bettler
11 **firmly established** fest etabliert
13 **to dress up** sich verkleiden
15 **to threaten** drohen
16 **to carve pumpkins** Kürbisse schnitzen

Detroit: The decline of an American city

Of the many cities in the United States that are shrinking in population, Detroit in Michigan is the hardest hit. At its high-point in the 1950s, Detroit was the car-
20 making capital of the world and had a population of 1.85 million people, making it the fourth largest city in the United States. Today, after losing out to the massive competition in the worldwide automobile industry, especially from Japan and Korea, the population is down to 700,000, leaving hundreds of thousands of abandoned homes in the city. About a third of Detroit's 360-km² area is either
25 vacant or derelict. In the golden age of the car in the 1950s and 60s, Detroit was home to the "Big Three" automobile companies: Ford, General Motors and Chrysler. Together they were the largest car-makers in the USA and Canada. Thousands of people worked in the car-making factories. People in Detroit had the highest per capita income in the entire USA. But soon the wealthier people
30 began to move out to the suburbs, taking their businesses with them, and the demographics of the city began to change. Riots in the late 1960s and the famous "Devil's Night" in the 1980s (arson attacks on the night before Halloween) led to an even greater population decline, increased poverty and a massive crime problem. Others cities which once had vibrant industrial economies and were
35 situated in what was in earlier times called the "Manufacturing Belt" or the "Factory Belt" are also shrinking. These include Pittsburgh, St. Louis (Missouri), Cleveland (Ohio), and even Washington D.C.

18 **to shrink** schrumpfen
19 **hit** betroffen
21 **to lose out** unterliegen
24 **abandoned** verlassen
25 **vacant** leer (stehend)
25 **derelict** verlassen
29 **per capita income** Pro-Kopf-Einkommen
30 **suburb** Vorstadt
31 **riots** Unruhen
32 **arson** Brandstiftung
33 **decline** Rückgang
34 **vibrant economy** boomende Wirtschaft
35 **situated** gelegen

Ziel: *setting the mood* – Einstimmung auf das Halloween-Thema und Antizipation der Geschichte zur Vorentlastung der Schreibaufgabe

Aufgabe 1: Die SuS betrachten die Bilder und äußern spontan ihre Assoziationen. Diese Runde sollte sehr schnell gehen, die Antworten sollten kurz und spontan sein. Jeder kann und soll sich hier äußern. Dann wird die Geschichte gelesen/gehört.

pre-reading
KV 10.1, Aufg. 1
ca. 5 min

Ziel: Sicherung des Textverständnisses

Aufgabe 2: Die SuS erzählen kurz Teile der Geschichte anhand der Bilder nach. Dabei können Fragen zum Textverständnis geklärt werden. Aufgabe 2 b) sollte als „Blitzlicht" durchgeführt werden, d. h. jede/r macht eine kurze Aussage zur Geschichte. Die Äußerungen werden nicht kommentiert.

post-reading
KV 10.1, Aufg. 2
ca. 5–10 min

Ziele: vertieftes Textverständnis, intensive Auseinandersetzung mit dem Text, Textbelege finden

Die SuS bearbeiten die Aufgaben 2 c) und 3 in Partnerarbeit. Anschließend werden die Ergebnisse im Klassenverband zusammengetragen.

Mögliche Erweiterung der Aufgabe 2 c): *Find hints in the text.*

KV 10.1, Aufg. 2c), 3
ca. 15–20 min

KV 10.2 erweitert jetzt den Rahmen auf das Genre der *horror / mystery story*.

Ziel: Wortschatzarbeit, *creative writing* (gelenkte Schreibaufgabe)

1. Schritt: Die SuS bereiten das *mind map* vor, indem sie das Muster unter 1 a) auf die Rückseite des Arbeitsblattes kopieren.
2. Schritt: Die SuS arbeiten arbeitsteilig in Gruppen. Jede Gruppe erhält ein Din-A3-Blatt, in das das Gruppenergebnis groß und leserlich eingetragen wird. Es wird vorher festgelegt, welche Wortart von welcher Gruppe gesucht wird, wobei die Wortarten *nouns* und *verbs* auch gern doppelt besetzt sein dürfen. Es gibt ein festes Zeitlimit von 10 Minuten – innerhalb dieser Zeit müssen mindesten zehn Wörter gefunden und in das A3-Blatt eingetragen werden. Dabei sollen die SuS – wenn möglich – unbedingt kleine Zeichnungen beifügen, bei unbekannten Wörtern muss die Übersetzung dabei stehen.
3. Schritt: Die Gruppen lassen ihr A3-Blatt auf dem Tisch liegen. Die SuS. bekommen jetzt 10 Minuten Zeit, alle Ergebnisse auf ihr eigenes Blatt zu übertragen und Zeichnungen hinzuzufügen. Sie gehen dabei von Tisch zu Tisch, mischen sich, zeigen sich ihre Ergebnisse usw.

KV 10.2, Aufg. 1a)
ca. 15–20 min
Material: A3-Papier, Wörterbuch oder Internetzugang

Tipp: Um sicherzustellen, dass alle Schüler/innen alle Wörter abgeschrieben haben, kann man am Ende zählen lassen, wie viele Wörter jeder hat und diese mit den Gruppenergebnissen abgleichen. Die A3-Blätter aus der Gruppenarbeit können im Klassenzimmer aufgehängt werden.

Aufgabe 1 b) eignet sich gut als Hausaufgabe, wobei die verwendeten Wörter farbig hervorgehoben werden sollten.

KV 10.2, Aufg. 1 b)

Ziel: extensives Lesen (*reading for fun*), Nacherzählen

Aufgabe 2 greift eine moderne Version der *horror / mystery story* auf: *urban legends*. Die SuS sollen hier viel lesen und stöbern. Wenn kein Internetzugang für jeden Schüler zur Verfügung steht, sollte eine große Auswahl dieser Geschichten ausgedruckt bereitgestellt werden (gern nach Kategorien geordnet). Die SuS wählen dann jeweils eine Geschichte aus und notieren diese in Stichwörtern. Anschließend erzählen sie ihre Geschichte frei (gern genretypisch) anhand der Stichwörter nach.

KV 10.2, Aufg. 2a/b
Vorbereitung: ca. 20 min
Erzählzeit: ca. 20 min
Material: Internetzugang für alle SuS oder Ausdrucke vieler „urban legends" von der Webseite

1. **Before you read the story:**

   Look at the four pictures. What do they make you think of?

2. **After you have read the story:**

   a) *Explain: how are the pictures you have just looked at related to the story?*

   b) *What is your first reaction to the story? Write one sentence.*

   _____

   c) *Can you think of a reason why the first-person narrator has this nightmare?*

   _____

   _____

   _____

3. **Reality or dream?**

   a) *Which parts in this story are clearly reality or clearly part of a dream? Which parts are unclear?*

Reality	Dream	Unclear

   b) *What effect does this have on the reader?*

1. **The story "13th Street" combines elements of horror and mystery.**

   a) *Get into groups and find at least ten words that a horror story or mystery story should contain[1]. Each group has to find words of a certain category (e.g. nouns, verbs...), then mix groups and exchange your words, so that you all have a mind map of spooky words. Use the back of this page for your mind map. It could look like this:*

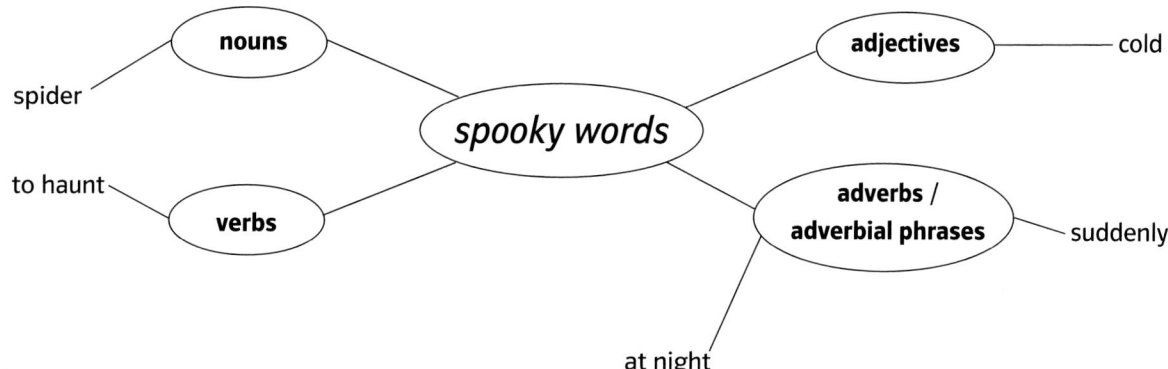

   b) *Now choose at least six of the words and write a horror or mystery story that contains all of these words. The story should not be about a dream. It should not contain any blood or severed[2] body parts. Try to create a scary atmosphere using mystery rather than violence. Write about 200–300 words.*

2. **The fascination of horror and mystery**

   Halloween is becoming more and more popular in Germany, too – and not only because of the sweets! We love getting dressed up, we are fascinated by the thrill of zombies, mummies and ghosts. But are these creatures just a figment of our imagination[3]? Do horror and mystery only exist in nightmares? There are stories that sound real. They have always happened to a friend of a friend. They are called *"urban legends"* or *"urban myths"*.

   Visit the following website: *http://urbanlegends.about.com* and read some of the stories. You can choose from a number of categories. Find **the scariest story** and **the most likely story to have really happened**. Take notes and tell the stories to your class in your own words.

I think... well... probably...
it happened to a friend of a friend...
or so I heard

A. This story is really true! Title of the story: _____

B. The scariest story I found! Title of the story: _____

[1] **to contain** *beinhalten*
[2] **severed** *abgetrennt*
[3] **figment of our imagination** *Phantasiegebilde, Produkt unserer Einbildung*

Servant of God by David Fermer

The turkey is ready. It's been in the oven for hours. The table is set. The whole family is here: Mom, Rachel, Caitlin; Uncle Joe and Aunt Theresa; Grandpa and Grandma. My little sisters even decorated the house. There are paper chains and balloons everywhere. It looks like someone's birthday party. There's only one

5 thing missing: Dad.

"You'd better take it out, darlin'! It's gonna be dry as a bone!"

Grandpa is right, but Mom is never going to take that turkey out of the oven before Dad gets here. She's been calling him all day, but his phone is off. He called home before leaving Houston this morning. He was ecstatic. "It's like Joel said," he

10 told Mom. "A full house last night! 17,000 people, all celebrating Jesus together! Praise the Lord!"

Joel Appleton is the pastor of Lakewater Church, the biggest church in Texas. He invited Dad to preach with him for Thanksgiving. Dad was never going to say no. Not to a congregation of 17,000. Our church in Little Rock only gets about a

15 thousand people a week, but Dad has big plans. He wants to build the first megachurch in Arkansas.

"He's probably just stuck in traffic," Grandma says. "You know what it's like on Thanksgiving. Everybody in America is on the road."

"So why's his cell phone off?" Mom says.

20 "Maybe his battery's dead," I suggest, but we all know that's not true. Dad could be out in the desert and he'd still find a way to charge his cell phone.

Eventually Mom does take the turkey out of the oven. We've just turned on the TV and are watching some movie to pass the time, when the doorbell rings. Everyone jumps to their feet. Mom opens the door, but it's not Dad. Instead two

25 cops are standing on the doorstep, their faces hidden behind sunglasses. "Mrs. Hillard?" asks the one standing in front.

Mom tries to say something, but she can't speak.

"Did something happen?" I ask next to Mom at the door. I just turned 17, and when Dad's away, I get to be the man in the house.

30 The cop takes a driver's license out of a wallet. Dad's wallet. "Is this your father?" he asks.

I look at Dad's pale face staring out from the card and nod.

"There was an accident," he explains.

"Oh my God!" Mom smothers her mouth with her hand. "Is he hurt?"

35 "No, ma'am. But a motorcyclist is dead."

"I don't understand. What does this have to do with my dad?" I ask.

"That's what we want to ask Mr. Hillard," says the police officer. "We found this wallet next to the bike. An unidentified man was seen leaving the scene of the accident in a hurry."

1 **turkey** *Truthahn*
1 **set** *gedeckt*
3 **paper chain** *Papierkette*
6 **gonna** *going to*
11 **praise the Lord!** *gelobt sei der Herr!*
13 **to preach** *predigen*
14 **congregation** *Kirchengemeinde*
21 **to charge** *aufladen*
30 **wallet** *Brieftasche*
32 **pale** *blass*
32 **to nod** *nicken*
33 **accident** *Unfall*
34 **to smother** *völlig bedecken*

40 The tears in Mom's eyes disappear instantly and are replaced by rage. "What are you trying to say, officer?" she cries. "Do you know who my husband is? Have you any idea who you are talking about here? My husband is a servant of God!"

"We know that, ma'am. But even pastors have accidents."

Mom is speechless. My little sisters cling to her legs and start crying, but
45 before anyone can speak again, Dad's Lincoln pulls up outside the house and Dad gets out of the car.

"Good afternoon, officers!" he says as he walks up the garden path as if he'd just gone out to buy some milk. "Is there a problem?"

Mom runs out to him. "Darling! These police officers … We were so worried
50 about you."

"You don't need to worry about me, honey." Then he sees his wallet in the police officer's hand. "Ah, you found it! That's terrific! Where was it?"

"On Route 45."

Dad holds out his hand and takes back the wallet. "Must have been stolen
55 from my hotel room this morning." After looking inside, he adds, "Gee, they didn't even take the cash. That's strange …"

"Mr. Hillard, were you on Route 45 today?" asks the cop.

"No, sir. I took the back route. The 190. Heard there'd been an accident on the radio."

60 My little sisters push past the cops and jump at Dad. "Hey, my little angels! Have you two been crying?" he asks and puts his arms around them.

Mom gives the police officers a look-to-kill and hisses, "You should be ashamed of yourselves, gentlemen! And that on Thanksgiving!"

She turns and walks past them into the house. Caitlin and Rachel drag Dad in
65 after her. "Thanks for dropping by, officers!" he says as he disappears into the house. "God be with you!"

I wait on the doorstep and watch the police officers go back to their patrol car. As they pull away, I notice a scratch on the side of the Lincoln. I go up to the car and bend down to look at it more closely. It wasn't there before Dad left for
70 Houston.

"Come on, big man! Let's get this party going!" Dad is standing at the front door, a glass of Coke in his hand. When he sees what I'm looking at, he steps out onto the lawn. "Some dumb kids fooling around in the city," he says. "I'll take it to the repair shop after the holiday."

75 He comes up to me and puts his hand on my shoulder. "Today is Thanksgiving, son," he says. "We gotta give thanks for what we have." He gently pulls me up to my feet. "Now how about we get us some of that sweet-smelling turkey before it gets cold? I don't know about you, but I'm starving!"

* * *

40 **tear** *Träne*
40 **instantly** *sofort*
40 **to replace** *ersetzen*
40 **rage** *Wut*
45 **to pull up** *anhalten* 52
   terrific *großartig*
62 **to hiss** *fauchen, zischen*
62 **to be ashamed** *sich schämen*
65 **to drop by** *vorbeikommen*
68 **scratch** *Kratzer*
69 **to bend down** *sich bücken*
69 **more closely** *genauer*
73 **lawn** *Rasen*
73 **to fool around** *Quatsch machen*
76 **gotta** *have got to*
78 **to starve** *verhungern*

Thanksgiving: Fourth Thursday in November

The fourth Thursday in November is a day when families all over the United States come together to celebrate Thanksgiving. Traditionally, people eat a large meal including turkey and watch a football game on TV. The first Thanksgiving was celebrated in 1621 in Massachusetts by a group of settlers who had come to
5 America from England. They were celebrating their first successful harvest, and the feast was said to have lasted for three days. A number of Native Americans also participated in this famous Thanksgiving, sharing the pilgrim's food of mashed potatoes, pumpkin pie and corn on the cob. But it wasn't until later that President Abraham Lincoln declared a national Thanksgiving Day in 1863. Since
10 then, Thanksgiving has been observed annually in the United States. Every year, millions of Americans travel many miles over the Thanksgiving holiday weekend to be with their family. The four- or five-day weekend is one of the busiest travel periods of the whole year. Another traditional part of Thanksgiving takes place at the White House. The President of the United States is presented with a turkey
15 from the National Turkey Federation which he "pardons" live on TV. The turkey is then allowed to live out its days on a historical farm. The other estimated 45 million turkeys are eaten later on the same day.

3 **turkey** *Truthahn*
5 **harvest** *Ernte*
6 **feast** *Festmahl*
7 **to participate** *teilnehmen*
7 **pilgrim** *Pilger*
8 **mashed potato** *Kartoffelbrei*
8 **pumpkin pie** *Kürbiskuchen*
8 **corn on the cob** *Maiskolben*
10 **annually** *jährlich*
15 **to pardon** *begnadigen*
16 **estimated** *geschätzt*

Hallelujah: Megachurches in the USA

America has always been a very religious country. The first European settlers
20 who came to the North American continent to start a new life often did so to escape religious persecution at home. They brought their faith with them and were able to practice their religion in freedom. They were Puritans, Quakers, Calvinists, and later Catholics from Protestant England. They built churches all over America, but it wasn't until more recently that pastors began to build
25 megachurches. A megachurch is a church which is attended by an average of more than 2,000 people every Sunday. There are approximately 1,300 megachurches in the United States. The phenomenon of megachurches is something that only developed since the start of the new millennium. The largest megachurch in the USA today is Lakewood Church in Houston, Texas, with more than 45,000 people
30 attending church every weekend. Megachurches are often criticized for taking members away from smaller, more community-based churches. They use highly professional stage performances, including dancing and music, to entertain the congregation. Megachurches are financed by donations from the congregation, so the more people you have in your church, the more money the church earns.
35 Many of the pastors of megachurches are rich, especially since their churches don't have to pay taxes.

21 **persecution** *Verfolgung*
21 **faith** *Glaube*
26 **approximately** *ungefähr*
32 **stage performance** *Bühnenaufführung*
32 **to entertain** *unterhalten*
33 **congregation** *Kirchengemeinde*
33 **donation** *Spende*
36 **tax** *Steuer*

Ziel: *Awareness*, Auseinandersetzung mit den moralischen Implikationen der Geschichte

Aufgabe 1: Die SuS erkunden zunächst ihr eigenes Gerechtigkeitsverständnis zu der Frage, wie kriminelle Taten berühmter Persönlichkeiten zu beurteilen sind. Sie vergleichen ihre Ergebnisse mit denen ihres Nachbarn / eines anderen Paares.

pre-reading
KV 11.1, Aufg. 1
ca. 15 min.

Ziel: Sicherung des Textverständnisses; einem Text Informationen entnehmen / Textbelege finden

Aufgabe 2 a/b: Die SuS bekommen ca. 10–15 Minuten Zeit, um die Geschichte für sich zu lesen und die Aufgaben 2 a) und b) in Einzelarbeit vorzubereiten. Es ist ebenfalls möglich, den Text zunächst nur hören zu lassen und dabei Aufgabe 2 a) als Hörverstehensaufgabe zu geben; anschließend wird dann der Text ausgeteilt und Aufgabe 2 b) mit dem Text gelöst. Zum Vergleich der Lösungen kann eine Folie vorbereitet werden.

while-reading
KV 11.1, Aufg. 2
ca. 15–20 min.

Für Gruppen, die sinnentnehmendes Lesen / *reports* weiter üben sollen, bietet sich folgende Hausaufgabe an:

mögliche Hausaufgabe

> **The accident**
> *What do we know about the accident? Write the police officers' report, which should contain the facts about "Who?", "What?", "Where?", "When?", "How?" and "Why?" as far as they are known.*

Das Aufgabenblatt KV 11.2 nähert sich jetzt verschiedenen Aspekten der Geschichte: Betrachtet werden dabei sowohl die Standpunkte und Handlungsweisen der einzelnen Figuren als auch der SuS.

Ziel: Vertiefung des Textverständnisses; Entwicklung einer eigenen Haltung; *creative writing*

Aufgaben 3 a), 4 und 5: Die SuS bearbeiten die Aufgaben 3 a), 4 und 5 in Partnerarbeit; die Lösungen werden im Klassenverband verglichen.

Mit Aufgabe 3 b) kann auf verschiedene Weisen verfahren werden:

a) Sie kann als Vorbereitung einer *debate* dienen – die SuS werden dazu in zwei Teams aufgeteilt und wählen / losen ihren Standpunkt. Sie bereiten ihre Eingangsreden und Argumente im Team vor (ca. 20 Minuten). Anschließend treten die Teams gegeneinander an (ca. 15 Minuten).

b) Die SuS bestimmen ihren Standpunkt selbst und schreiben eine kurze Rede (ca. 20 Minuten). Dann treten jeweils zwei Schüler, ein „Verteidiger" und ein „Staatsanwalt", gegeneinander an – die Gruppe fungiert jeweils als „Jury" und entscheidet anhand der Reden über Schuld und Unschuld (ca. 15 Minuten).

post-reading
KV 11.2, Aufg. 3–5
insgesamt ca. 50–55 min.

Homework: *Choose **one** of three possible tasks.*

a) The first-person narrator decides to confide in his grandfather and ask him for help. *Write the dialogue.*

b) The first-person narrator can't talk to anybody, so he writes about his feelings and his problem in his diary. *Write this diary entry.*

c) The first-person narrator needs to ask an adult for advice but doesn't know who to turn to. In the end, he writes a letter to the agony aunt of a teen magazine who promises to help teenagers. *Write his letter and her reply.*

1. **Before you read the story** *Think! Pair! Share!*

   Imagine the following situation: Two people commit the same crime (e.g. stealing an expensive jacket from a shop or beating somebody up), one of them is an ordinary citizen, the other person is a celebrity. Make up your mind about the following two questions:

   a) If a celebrity commits a crime is it worse than if the criminal was an ordinary person?

   b) Should a celebrity be punished more severely for committing crimes than ordinary people?

   Study the following hypothetical cases and decide. Give reasons (keywords only):

The criminal is a(n) ...	a) Is this person's crime worse than if an ordinary person had committed it? Why (not)?	b) Should this person be punished more severely than an ordinary person? Why (not)?
actor / actress or singer		
famous football player or boxer		
politician		

   Now compare your solution with that of your neighbor and discuss them. If possible, agree on a solution. Next find another couple and discuss your results with them. If possible, agree on a solution.

2. **While you are reading the story: The family**

   a) Find information about the family.

Family name:	Family members:
Father's profession:	Where do they live:

   b) Find proof in the text that...

   ... this family is very religious.

   _____ (ll.   )

   _____ (ll.   )

   ... this family is very traditional.

   _____ (ll.   )

   _____ (ll.   )

3. A question of guilt

The crime Mr. Hillard is being accused of is called *hit and run*; it means a driver has caused an accident and has then left the scene of the accident.

a) Find hints in the text that …

… the father is innocent.	… the father is guilty.

b) Make up your mind: Is Mr. Hillard guilty of committing a case of "hit and run" or not?
Imagine you are either his lawyer or the public prosecutor. Write a speech to convince the jury of your point of view that he is innocent / guilty of the crime.

4. The police officers

a) What did the police officers do?

_____

_____

_____

b) What do you think they should have done if they had done their duty?

_____

_____

_____

c) Why didn't they do their duty?

_____

_____

_____

5. The first-person narrator & his family

Use a separate piece of paper to answer the following questions:

a) How does the first-person narrator feel at the end of the story? Why?

b) What would you advise him to do?

African Roots by David Fermer

"Brothers, sisters, fellow African-Americans, welcome!"

The hall was full of people as his mother pushed him gently through the door. The air smelled of cigarettes and sweat. Men in black suits and open-necked
5 shirts stood against the walls. Women in colorful kaftans, their heads wrapped in scarves, were seated in rows, fanning their faces with pieces of paper. Christmas had only just passed, but here in Hawaii there was no such thing as snow.

The man on the stage raised his arms into the air. "Today is a day for you all." He spoke like a song. "A day to celebrate who you are and where you come from."

10 The boy's mother bent down and whispered into his ear: "I have to go to the restroom. I'll be back in a minute." She pointed to an empty seat next to an old man with curly white hair. The boy sat down obediently. As he watched his mother leave the room, he couldn't help noticing she was the only white person in attendance.

15 "We must learn to be proud of our African roots", said the man on the stage. "Black is beautiful. Black is good."

It was only since returning from Indonesia last year, in the summer of '71, that the boy had started to notice the color of people's skin. Toot and Gramps were white like his Mom. His stepfather, Lolo, was Indonesian, and had smooth
20 chocolaty skin. His biological father was from Kenya and had dark brown skin like the ebony keys of a piano. His half-sister, Maya, who'd been born in Indonesia and was now two years old, was a lovely olive color. But here in the hall everyone was black. Like him.

"We are no longer the white man's slave," the speaker on the stage said. "We
25 do not have to do the jobs he does not want to do. We do not have to cross the street when we see him walking towards us. And we do not have to celebrate his festivals. We have our own."

"Kwanzaa!" cried someone in the audience.

The speaker nodded. "That's right! Kwanzaa belongs to us only! It is our
30 festival, not like the white man's Christmas. This is why we started Kwanzaa six years ago. For our communities. For our families. For our culture! Seven days, like the harvest festivals in Africa, to celebrate who we are and where we come from!"

The people in the audience clapped and cheered and cried out "Kwanzaa! Kwanzaa!" as the man on the stage took a watermelon from a table of fruit and
35 began to cut it into slices and pass it around. Men began singing at the back of the hall while the women at the front stood up and went onto the stage to help serve the fruit.

The old man sitting next to the boy turned to him and smiled. "His words are true, you know," he said. "You must always be proud of where you come from."

1 **root** *Wurzel*
2 **fellow** *Mit-*
3 **gently** *sanft*
6 **row** *Reihe*
6 **to fan** *fächeln*
10 **to bend down** *sich bücken*
11 **restroom** *Toilette*
12 **obediently** *gehorsam*
14 **to be in attendance** *anwesend*
21 **ebony** *Ebenholz*
24 **slave** *Sklave*
29 **to belong** *gehören*
32 **harvest** *Ernte*
35 **slice** *Scheibe*

40　The boy noticed that the man's front teeth were missing. "I am."

"That's good. How old are you, boy?"

"Eleven."

"Well! Almost a man! How do you like Kwanzaa, my friend?"

"I like the music and the clothes, and the fruit looks fine."

45　The old man nodded. "Oh yes! The fruit is the best. This island is good to us all – black, white or Asian. We all love the fruit!"

The speaker from the stage came up to them, holding out a bowl of sliced watermelon. "Take!" he said. "This is the harvest of our people."

The boy waited until the old man had taken a slice of melon, then he helped 50　himself. "Thank you."

After the speaker had moved on, the old man took a bite of his melon and said, "Mr. Karenga is a fine speaker."

"I'm in the debate team at school," the boy replied.

"Fine! Fine! Maybe one day you'll be an important man like Mr. Karenga."

55　"Yes," said the boy, wiping away the melon's juice which was trickling down his chin. "I want to become president."

The man coughed as if he'd just choked on his watermelon. "You want to become president?" he cried, laughing. "The president of what? The school debate team?"

60　"No. Of the United States of America."

The old man must have seen the seriousness in the boy's eyes, because this time he didn't laugh. He just stared at the boy, open-mouthed, silent. The boy could see the wet watermelon on his tongue.

"But … but this is not possible," the old man stammered. "Look in the mirror, 65　my boy. No black man will ever be president of this country."

A woman standing behind the old man must have overheard the conversation. She turned and clapped her hands together, crowing like a cockerel. "A black president?! What will they think of next?"

Soon everyone around them was laughing. Men were slapping each other on 70　the shoulder. Women giggled into their hands. "An African-American president? And pigs can fly!" Only the old man did not laugh. He remained perfectly still, watching the boy through his tired eyes. "A black president? You have quite an imagination, my boy!"

It was with some relief that the boy saw his mother come back into the room. 75　She was pushing her way through the crowd, looking for him. She found him at the center of the laughter.

"Is everything okay?" she asked, looking into the laughing faces around her. "Why is everyone laughing, Barack? What have you done? What's so funny, Barack? Tell me!"

* * *

---

51 **to take a bite** *abbeißen*
55 **to wipe** *wischen*
56 **chin** *Kinn*
57 **to cough** *husten*
57 **to choke** *ersticken*
61 **seriousness** *Ernsthaftigkeit*
64 **to stammer** *stottern*
66 **to overhear** *zufällig mithören*
67 **cockerel** *Hahn*
69 **to slap** *klopfen*
70 **to giggle** *kichern*
71 **to remain** *bleiben*
73 **imagination** *Fantasie*
74 **relief** *Erleichterung*

Kwanzaa: December 26th

Kwanzaa is a seven-day festival that was started in 1966 to celebrate African heritage in the USA. It was the first specifically African-American holiday. The man who started it was called Maulana Karenga. Karenga was an activist who fought for the rights of black people in the USA. Up until the 1960s, African-Americans did
5 not enjoy the same rights as their fellow citizens all over America. Particularly in the states in the south, African-Americans were treated as second-class citizens. They didn't have equal job opportunities and in some states they couldn't even vote. They often had to sit at the back of the bus or use a separate entrance when going to the cinema. There were even "colored only" drinking fountains and
10 sections at baseball games. Karenga and other civil rights activists like Martin Luther King, Jr. or Malcolm X believed that black people in America had forgotten to be proud of their culture. Kwanzaa was a means for African-Americans to reconnect to their African roots, giving blacks an opportunity to celebrate themselves and their history. The name Kwanzaa comes from the Swahili and
15 means "first fruits of the harvest". The week-long festival lasts from December 26th to January 1st and is celebrated in America by an estimated 5 to 30 million people.

2 **heritage** *Erbe*
4 **rights** *Rechte*
5 **fellow citizen** *Mitbürger*
5 **particularly** *besonders*
7 **equal opportunities** *Chancengleichheit*
12 **means** *Mittel, Weg*
13 **root** *Wurzel*
15 **harvest** *Ernte*
16 **to estimate** *schätzen*

Barack Obama: The first black president

Barack Obama is the physical embodiment of multicultural America and the
20 "American Dream". His mother was a white American of English descent, his father from Kenya. Obama was born in Hawaii in 1961, where he lived for the first eight years of his life. His parents divorced when he was two years old, and when his mother married again, this time an Indonesian, Obama moved to Indonesia and lived there until coming back to Hawaii when he was ten. His half-sister,
25 Maya, was born in Indonesia. Obama was a child during the Civil Rights Movement of the 1960s, when black and white people took to the streets all over America to protest against racial inequality. Obama was only two when the great civil rights activist Martin Luther King, Jr. gave his "I have a dream" speech at the Lincoln Memorial in Washington, D.C. In this masterpiece of public speaking, King, a
30 pastor of the church, called on the American people to look beyond the color of people's skin. "I have a dream … that my four little children will one day live in a nation where they will not be judged by the color of their skin, but by the content of their character." Without the hard work and the sacrifices made by the civil rights activists of the 1960s, no African-American could ever have become
35 President of the United States. This finally happened, for the first time in U.S. history, on January 20, 2009, when Barack Obama was sworn in as the nation's 44th President.

19 **embodiment** *Inbegriff*
20 **descent** *Herkunft*
25 **civil rights movement** *Bürgerrechtsbewegung*
27 **racial inequality** *rassenbedingte Ungleichheit*
29 **masterpiece** *Meisterwerk*
30 **to look beyond** *über etw. hinausschauen*
32 **to judge** *beurteilen*
32 **content** *Inhalt*
33 **sacrifice** *Opfer*
36 **to swear in** *vereidigen*

Ziel: *Awareness*, Auseinandersetzung mit Grenzen eigener Zukunftsträume
Aufgabe 1: Die SuS beschreiben ihre eigenen großen Träume und Hoffnungen und überprüfen sie auf ihre Umsetzbarkeit. Anschließend wird die Geschichte gelesen und gehört. Verständnisfragen werden im Klassenrahmen geklärt. Danach kann ein erneuter Blick auf die eigenen Träume geworfen werden, z. B. als Murmelphase.

pre-reading
KV 12.1, Aufg. 1
ca. 15 min.

Ziel: Kenntnisse über die Geschichte der Afro-Amerikaner und deren Kampf um Freiheit und Gleichberechtigung als historischer und literarischer Hintergrund
Aufgabe 2 a/b: Die SuS bekommen ca. 40 Minuten Zeit, um die Aufgaben 2a) und b) in Gruppenarbeit vorzubereiten. Die Gruppen arbeiten arbeitsteilig. Die Präsentation soll 3–5 Minuten nicht überschreiten.

post-reading
KV 12.1, Aufg. 2
Vorbereitungszeit ca. 40 min.
Präsentationszeit ca. 35 min.

Gruppe 1: Die Gruppe benutzt das große Plakatpapier und erstellt das *wall display* – ein Plakat mit einem großen Baum, in das auch die anderen Gruppen ihre Lösungen hineinkleben. Sie verwendet für ihre Zeichnung KV 12.2 als Vorlage und trägt die einzelnen Stationen stichwortartig ein (s. Lösung S. 87). Die Aufgabe dieser Gruppe ist es, die einzelnen Stationen inhaltlich vorzubereiten, einen Überblick im Sinne einer *timeline* zu geben, aber nicht inhaltlich in die Tiefe zu gehen (mögliche Informationen hierzu unter *http://www.infoplease.com/spot/bhmtimeline.html*). Diese Gruppe wird vermutlich Hilfe benötigen, um sich zu organisieren. Bei schwächeren Lerngruppen ist es auch möglich, dieser Gruppe die Lösung zur Verfügung zu stellen.

Material: KV 12.2, Zeichenpapier oder rotes, rundes Papier, großes Papier (Rolle oder Plakat), dicke Stifte, Scheren, Kleber

Gruppen 2–6: Sie finden die wesentlichen Punkte über ihr Thema heraus und schreiben diese in Stichpunkten auf Zeichenpapier. Dieses darf gern die Form eines Apfels annehmen, so dass die einzelnen Gruppenergebnisse als „Früchte" auf die Plakatvorlage geklebt werden können. Das Ergebnis ist ein großes Poster, das die Schritte der Emanzipation der Afro-Amerikaner in den USA als Baum nachzeichnet. Wichtig ist, dass die Gruppen nicht zu kleinschrittig arbeiten. Die Präsentationszeit von 3–5 Minuten soll auf gar keinen Fall überschritten werden.
Mögliche Quellen:
- http://en.wikipedia.org/wiki/Alex_Haley
- http://blogs.wsj.com/speakeasy/2013/10/23/what-really-became-of-solomon-northup-after-his-12-years-a-slave/
- http://www.thekingcenter.org/about-dr-king
- http://www.biography.com/people/nelson-mandela-9397017#synopsis&awesm=~oFJyZPOGQpn9Ep
- http://www.biography.com/people/barack-obama-12782369#awesm=~oFJzCUVPlp4MeR

Wie bei den vorherigen Vorschlägen lassen sich Biographien für alle Namen unter dem Reiter *Persons* auf der Webseite *http://www.biography.com* finden.
Die Gruppe 7 ist optional, abhängig von Klassengröße und Interessenlage der SuS. Ihre „Äpfel" sollten zur jeweiligen historischen Zeit passend angebracht werden.

Internetzugang nötig!!
Falls kein Internetzugang vorhanden ist, sollten die Informationen der angegebenen Webseiten (ggf. in gekürzter Form) mehrfach ausgedruckt werden.

Ziel: *Transfer* Bezug des Begriffs *American Dream* auf Barack Obama und andere
Die Aufgabe sollte als Hausaufgabe vorbereitet werden, die Diskussion erfolgt in der darauf folgenden Stunde.

KV 12.1, Aufg. 3

1. **Before you read the story:**

   a) Imagine, you could become anyone or anything you wanted to be: what / who would you like to be? A famous football player? A fashion model? A king or queen? The German Chancellor? *Tell your partner.*

   • What is your biggest dream? What would you have to do to make it come true? How realistic is it?

   b) How about these dreams? *Finish the following sentences:*

   I could / couldn't become the Pope, because _____

   _____

   I could / couldn't become the King / Queen of England, because _____

   _____

   I could / couldn't become Germany's next Superstar or Top Model, because _____

   _____

   c) **After reading the story:** Now look at your own hopes and dreams again. Has this story in any way influenced how you think about them? Explain why / why not?

2. **The American Dream – also for *Black People*?**

   a) What is "the American Dream"?
   Read http://america.day-dreamer.de/pro.htm and describe it in your own words.

   b) "From slave to millionaire?"
   Group work: *Work in groups of three to five. Make a brief (i.e. short!) presentation (no longer than 3–5 min.). Draw an apple and cut it out. Note down the most important points about your topic. You may add a picture if available. Then stick your apple on the tree which the first group has prepared as a wall display.*

   Group 1 The history of Afro-Americans: *Briefly present the big steps of the history of Afro-Americans to the class and prepare the wall display of the tree, using the following terms: Life in Africa – slavery – segregation – apartheid in South Africa – civil rights movement – the first black president of the United States – equality.*

   Group 2 "Roots" Alex Haley's Kunta Kinte: *Briefly present Alex Haley's semi-biographical story "Roots", which tells the story of his alleged African ancestor Kunta Kinte, and the miniseries that was made from it. What is the story about?*

   Group 3 Solomon Northup, the real story behind "Twelve years a slave": *Briefly present the real story behind the Oscar-winning movie "Twelve years a slave": the life of Solomon Northup.*

   Group 4 The fight for equality, Dr. Martin Luther King: *Briefly explain the role of Dr. Martin Luther King and his famous speech "I have a dream" for the civil rights movement.*

   Group 5: Apartheid in South Africa: *Nelson Mandela: Briefly explain what apartheid means and who Nelson Mandela was.*

   Group 6 The first black president of the United States, Barack Obama: *Briefly present the life of Barack Obama and why his role is so important to Afro-Americans.*

   Group 7 Which role did women play in the struggle for freedom and equality? (Harriet Beecher-Stowe, Harriet Tubman, Sojourner Truth, Ida B. Wells, Rosa Parks): *Briefly present the life of some of these women and the role they played in the Afro-American struggle for equality.*

3. **Discussion: Who of the above people has lived "his" (or "her") version of the American Dream?**

Copy the results of the goup work here:

EQUALITY

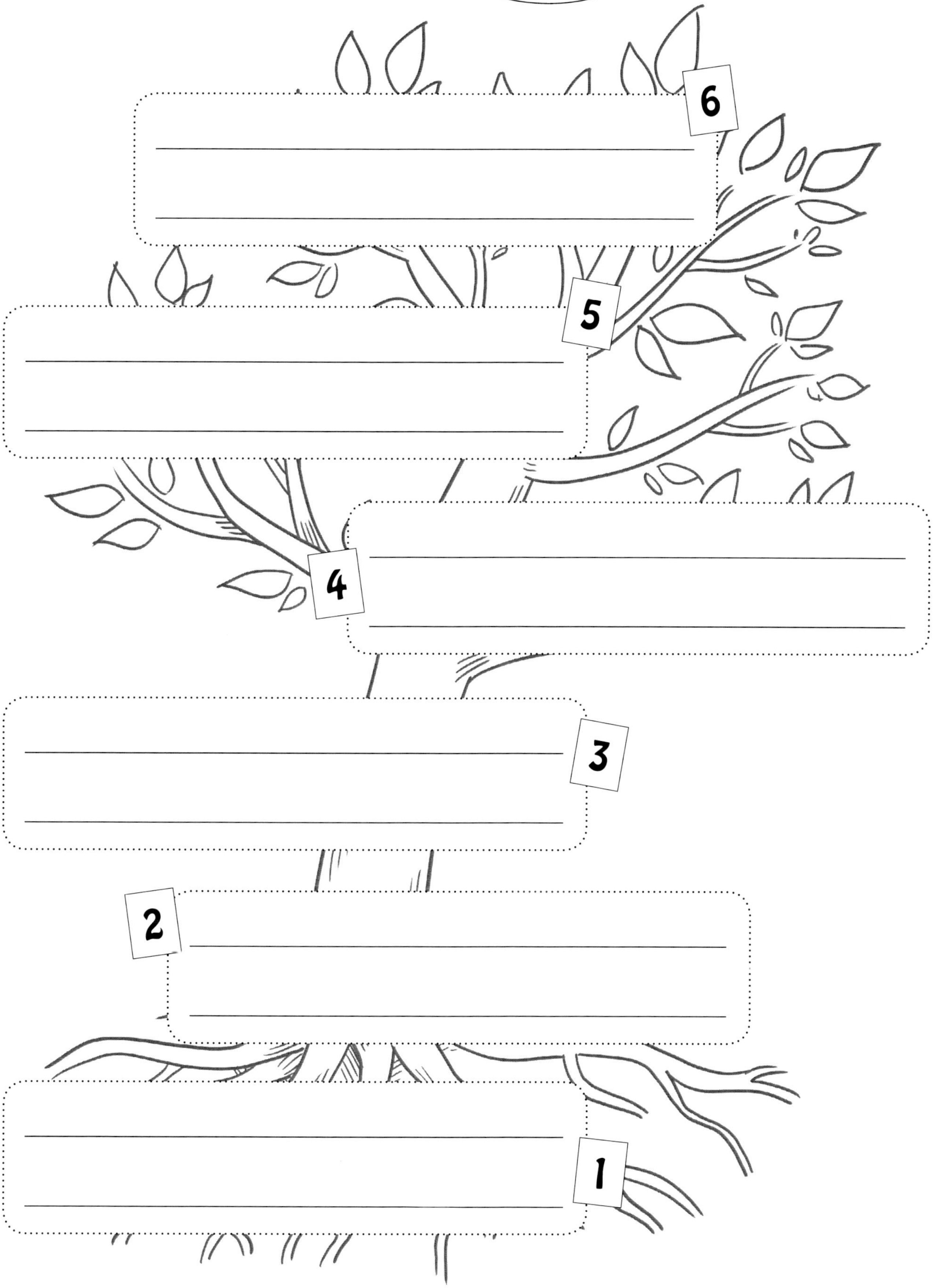

6
_____
_____

5
_____
_____

4
_____
_____

3
_____
_____

2
_____
_____

1
_____
_____

Lösungen

1 Will you be my Valentine?

Anschlussaufgabe / Hausaufgabe: *Possible solution*

Happy: Although Claire does not want to go out with Mitch she is nice to him. She tells him that she appreciates the effort he made for her and gives him hope by saying *"Maybe next year."*

Sad: Mitch likes Claire and he wants to go out with her, but she turns him down.

Differenzierungsaufgabe 1

Hints that Mitch might be "different": Mitch didn't understand why they always laughed so much. Watching and listening was far more interesting. Mitch was an expert at that. He'd been watching and listening all his life. (ll. 10–13); Mitch was terrible at Math. He just couldn't get his head around it. Numbers were fine as long as they followed each other in the correct order – 1, 2, 3, 4, 5, etc. – but as soon as the order changed, as soon as Mr. Alvarez told them to do things with numbers that didn't follow that order, Mitch didn't know what to do. (ll. 28–32); He knew he'd get there before her, even though it wasn't easy for him to run so fast. He almost fell over a couple of times. (ll. 50–51)

KV 1.1

Aufgabe 1: beste Antwort 4)

2 Forgiving Katrina

KV 2.1

Aufgabe 2: *Possible solution (sentences to underline)*

But as the storm raged over the city and the levees broke, flooding the streets; The city was in ruins. There was no running water, no electricity. Drinking water and food were contaminated. It was as if the storm had sucked New Orleans in, chewed on it and spit it out. The National Guard had come, rescued people, and started an evacuation; to find their house smelling of rot. The water, which had come up to the ceiling, was now gone, but the damage could be seen everywhere. The wooden floor was black with mud. Mold was eating away at the wallpaper. The colors had washed out of the family photographs hanging in the living room. Outside, the street was a river of rubble. It was as if someone had tipped a gigantic bucket of mud over their neighborhood. It took them months to clean up; How could a city which had been brought to its knees by Hurricane Katrina stand up and party? Only four months after the terrible storm, Mardi Gras took place.

KV 2.2

Aufgabe 1 Hurricane Katrina caused a lot of damage in New Orleans, for example hundreds of thousands were left without access to their homes or jobs, people (even children) were separated from family members and suffered both physical and mental distress. Many had lost their income and their homes.

President Bush was criticized for his behavior during the crisis because he did not return to Washington from his holiday. Also he didn't heed any warnings before the storm hit and he did not mention the amount of human suffering or any short-comings of how Katrina was dealt with.

The Federal Emergency Management Agency, whose job it is to organize help in case of a disaster, was criticized heavily for their slow reaction and their inability to coordinate efforts with other federal agency relief organizations.

The local government did not do a good job. They failed to execute the New Orleans disaster plan. Also there were lootings and the levees had been neglected.

A lot of people talked of discrimination because they assumed there was such a slow response to the disaster due to the fact that 2/3 of the residents of New Orleans are black and New Orleans is one of America's poorest cities. Within the city the poorest people – mostly African-Americans – were living in the lowest parts that were hit worst.

3 Opa Joe

KV 3.1

Aufgabe 2

Chasoret: chopped apples and ground nuts mixed with cinnamon and wine – symbol for the mortar the Jews used for building the pyramids when they were Egyptian slaves

Zeroa: bone of meat cooked in the oven – represents God's arm, punishing the Egyptians

Karpas: potatoes in salt water – represents the tears of the Jews

Aufgabe 3a)

– enslavement of the Jews in Egypt	– born in Germany, Opa Joe was sent to a concentration camp in Poland together with his family
– God inflicting plagues among the Egyptians, e.g. killing their first-born children	– (Opa Joe never gave up hope "But life always goes on, meydl, even from the darkest point ..." (ll. 25–27), because he had met his wife in a concentration camp.)
– the escape under the leadership of Moses	– immigrated to America in 1946 (ll. 14–15)
– birth of a nation	– raised a family (possibly in Brooklyn)
– Passover reminds the Jews of where they come from, "the birth of a nation from the chain of suffering"	– the tattoo reminds Opa Joe of his time of suffering at the hands of the Nazis (ll. 54 ff)

Aufgabe 3

b) *Possible solutions*

Again parallelism seems to be a structural element: Lisa is worried about her mother's illness and what it could mean to the family and her own future if her mother died of cancer. The suffering of her people, of Opa Joe, her mother's suffering and her own uncertain future all seem to add up and it all makes her very sad. But then she sees her new neighbors from Israel (representing her people) – they have children, they have a future; she sees her own family, there is her father presiding over the family, caring for them – they have a future; and there is the neighbor's son, who seems to like her – her own happy future is hinted at here. Opa Joe had also met his future wife when everything seemed dark and hopeless, yet he remained optimistic throughout his life – and now so does she.

4 ABC

KV 4.2

Aufgabe 1

a) *San Francisco:* melting pot of cultures – largest population of Chinese-Americans in the USA

James' life in San Francisco: he blended in and was accepted, he was nothing unusual, the fact that he was an ABC wasn't important

Casper: small town in Wyoming – only 50,000 inhabitants, all white

James' life in Casper: things were different, he stuck out like a sore thumb

b James sees himself as *American*:

– "he wasn't aware that he was different", – "James knew he looked Asian, but he didn't feel Asian at all." – "He spoke like an American." – "He played baseball like an American." – "He listened to American music, wore the same clothes as all the other kids in high school, and had the same dreams." – "The fact that he was an "ABC", an American-born Chinese, wasn't important at all."

c) He comes from an (upper) middle class background ("His father, an engineer, took on a three-year-contract for the Sinclair Oil Corporation"), big city kid ("San Francisco, on the Pacific Coast, is a true melting pot of cultures"), high school education ("his first day at his new high school"), athlete ("He played baseball like an American"), "James was a likeable guy, smart, sporty, down to earth"

Aufgabe 2

	a) first reaction	b) after a while	c) possible reaction to what happened
Ryan	– pretended to be his friend, but really planned to play an evil trick on him (ll. 21–27)	– didn't like James at all (ll. 40–42)	✕
other kids	– on the first day they treated him with respect because of Ryan (ll. 23–24) – but they also wanted to test the new boy (ll. 17–18) – after the prank they were sceptical for a while (ll. 51–53)	– after a while he was well liked (ll. 42–44)	– Kirsty might support him, as she helped him to play this prank and because she likes him – the other kids might be on his side, because Ryan was the school bully who had made everybody's life miserable – they might also be shocked at the outcome of this prank
teachers / principal	– after the prank they thought he was a drug-dealing kid from the ghetto (ll. 37–38), (ll. 51–53)	– after a while they liked him (l. 44)	– the principal / teachers would never be able to accept a student who had killed another student, even if it was an accident
other people from Casper	– at first they were rather sceptical, because he looked different (ll. 12–13)	– after a while James and his family were welcome – people invited them for meals and were invited back (ll. 45–47)	– they might feel sorry for James' parents, because they liked them – they might also return to their original hostility

5 Escape to the USA

KV 5.1

Aufgabe 2

Time: May 9th, 9 pm; **Place:** the U.S.-Mexican border; **Father:** stays in Mexico, calls his son *hijo gringo*, helps his son to get across the border in hope of a better future for his son; **Son:** 14, was chosen to try to get to the U.S. because he can speak English, hopes to be able to go to high school; **Cousin:** Miguel, has been living in the States for years, whether legally is unclear

Aufgabe 3

advantages: safety from violence and being killed by the drug cartels, hopes for a better future (ll. 18–21), a better education (ll. 49–50)

risks: danger of being caught by the U.S. border control guards (ll. 14–15), danger of being robbed, raped or killed by the banditos (ll. 31–32)

KV 5.2

Aufgabe 4 *Hilfreiche Textstellen, die auf die Liebe des Vaters zu seinem Sohn hinweisen:*

"Suerte, mi hijo. Good luck, my son, my father says to me" (l. 40); "I look at my father and see sadness in his eyes" (ll. 41–42); "Cuidado. Be careful, he says to me as we stand up" (l. 51); "He just stays there, kneeling by the hole in the fence, tears in his eyes." (ll. 64–65); "Corre, hijo. Corre. Run, my son, run. You know where you have to go. Live long. I love you. Your mother loves you, too." (ll. 67–68); "He did this for me, his hijo gringo, his American son." (l. 78)

6 Divided Country

KV 6.1

Aufgabe 2

Across: 2. cemetery, 4. fallen, 6. sword, 7. march, 8. grave, 9. battle

Down: 1. defeat, 2. civil war, 3. uniform, 5. combat

Aufgabe 4

a) *Possible solution:* The boys could have told their parents or teachers about the sword. The sword could have been given to a museum. The legally correct solution would have been to hand over the sword to the police. They might have gotten a reward (not guaranteed). They would certainly have been mentioned in the local newspapers.

b) *Possible solution:* Germany made a conscious effort to eliminate the worship of war heroes after WWII. We do not glorify our past but rather look at it as a history to learn from. Therefore German children do not usually re-enact war scenes. Germany's past as a divided country likewise does not play a major role anymore: to older people it may still be a painful memory, but to younger people it does not matter in their daily lives. It has not entered children's games.

In the U.S. the memory of past wars (the War of Independence, the Civil War, WW I and II) is kept alive. Arlington cemetery and Memorial Day are symbols of a culture that sees the military and the reverence of fallen soldiers in a much more positive light than our society.

7 Freedom

KV 7.1

Aufgabe 2

age: 19; **place of residence**: Dayton Correctional Institution; **family background**: father left family, mother drug addict; **education**: truant, stopped going to school at age 12, **criminal record**: aged 15: theft, aged 16: first time in juvenile prison, aged 17: 2nd time in juvenile prison, aged 18: 19 months in prison.

Aufgabe 3

a) wrong street name, cashier a man, robbers: two men and a woman, missing masks, weapons: baseball bats and knives, Eezi wears boots, nobody was hurt. b) They didn't turn off the CCTV camera; Eezi wore new trainers, which he had bought locally, he had left his name/address because of a contest.

Aufgabe 4

a) regular meals, a place to sleep, social contacts, a structured life, work, sb who looks after him / tells him what to do (andere Lösungen möglich).

b) He wanted to go back to prison.

c) His experiences of life outside prison are negative, he has no positive social relationships, no money / job, no education or perspective for a positive future (ll. 20–21, 23, 51–54). So far his life in prison has been better than his life on the outside. Life outside prison probably scares him.

d) The irony is that he may be free on Independence Day, but he is definitely not independent; freedom does not mean independence for him.

e) He apologizes to the lady, he has no intention of harming anybody (toy gun).

8 Patriot

KV 8.1

Aufgabe 1

a) *Lösungsvorschlag:* A racist is a person who believes that a particular race is superior to another. A liar is a person who does not tell the truth.

Aufgabe 2 *right:* 1, 5, *wrong:* 2, 4, 6, 8, 9, *not in the text:* 3, 7

Aufgabe 3 *Carmen's father:* Dominican Republic / cleaner at the WTC / hated America, considered Americans as economic colonialists / felt like a second-class citizen, found his job degrading

Carmen's mother: Dominican Republic / works in a supermarket / not in the text, but apparently did not share her husband's beliefs / not in the text, but apparently did not share her husband's beliefs

Carmen: New York, USA / still at school / loves America / has never experienced racism, does not feel poor

9 Indian Elvis

KV 9.1

Aufgabe 2 *Possible solution:* hair gel / pomade (l. 49), an Elvis record, an Indian drum – things which show that he lived in the white man's world of his own choice, but missed his cultural roots. Becoming Elvis did not mean denying his origins, but his people did not allow him to be a part of both worlds. Lines that show his regret: "You sometimes do crazy things" – "more than I ever imagined", "I had a great life, but I never stopped missing my people.", "I want to die among my own people."

KV 9.2
Aufgabe 2

a) white settlers took their land (l. 11), they nearly killed them off (l. 11), they put them in reservations, on land which was of no interest to them because there was no water / no natural resources (ll. 14–16)

b) *individuelle Lösungen, die in etwa folgende Aspekte enthalten könnten:* **Oil / Gas Drilling on Reservations:** *advantages:* money and jobs, Native Americans who had left move back; *disadvantages:* pollution, contradicts traditional beliefs
   The Lives of young Native Americans: alarmingly high rate of teen suicides on reservations due to poverty, unemployment, domestic violence, sexual assault, alcoholism and drug addiction

10 13th Street

KV 10.1
Aufgabe 2

c) The first-person narrator lies to her parents about wanting to go trick-or-treating. She even thinks it's funny that they believe her – she intends to go to a party (ll. 19–22). But apparently she is not as cool as she thinks: lying to her parents weighs on her conscience and she has a nightmare about breaking another promise she gave them (ll. 12–18). In the end she realizes she had this nightmare because she lied to her parents (l. 77).

Aufgabe 3

a) Reality: (ll. 1–23), (ll. 74–77)
   Dream: (ll. 70–74: …my dad.) In these lines the nightmarish atmosphere is rather obvious, but the reader cannot be fully sure until he reads "and suddenly I was sitting in my bed". It can be argued that a certain unrealistic, dreamlike atmosphere starts from "We turn around and see him" (l. 63). Unclear: (ll. 24–69)

b) The nightmare connects to the beginning of the story. Also it starts off in a very realistic way, the change in atmosphere is very gradual. The reader realizes only in hindsight that he has been reading the description of a nightmare, so the end comes as a surprise.

11 Servant of God

KV 11.1
Aufgabe 2

a) *Family name:* Hillard; *Family members:* Mr. and Mrs. Hillard (Dad and Mom), first-person narrator (their son), Rachel and Caitlin (their daughters), Uncle Joe and Aunt Theresa, Grandpa and Grandma; *Father's profession:* pastor / preacher, *live in:* Little Rock, Arkansas

b) The family is very religious: (ll. 10–11), (l. 42)
   The family is very traditional: (ll. 7–8); (ll. 28–29)

KV 11.2

Aufgabe 3

a) ... *father is innocent:* he claims his wallet had been stolen in the hotel, he did not take Route 45, because he had heard about an accident on the radio, a kid scratched his car when he was in the city.

... *father is guilty:* his wallet was found at the site of the accident, next to the bike, he claims somebody stole his wallet, but neither his money nor his driver's license are missing, there is a new scratch on the side of his car, which he wants to get repaired as soon as possible.

Aufgabe 4

a) They inform Mrs. Hillard of an accident involving a motorcyclist and an unknown man and ask her about her husband's whereabouts as they found his wallet beside the bike. They give the wallet back to Mr. Hillard and ask him whether he took Route 45, where the accident happened.

b) They should have looked at his car and questioned him about the scratches. They should have asked for proof.

c) One can only assume that the fact that he is a "servant of God" (l. 42), i.e. a pastor, induces the policemen to simply take his word for it without asking for proof. Mrs. Hillard heightens this feeling further by appealing to their sense of propriety and their conscience ("You should be ashamed of yourselves, gentlemen. And that on Thanksgiving.", ll. 62–63)

Aufgabe 5

a) The author does not tell us directly how the first-person narrator feels, but we can deduct from his thoughts when he sees the scratch ("It wasn't there before Dad left for Houston.", ll. 69–70) that he is wondering whether his dad told the policemen the truth. He seems to doubt his father's word, otherwise he would not have paid any attention to the scratch, therefore he might also doubt his father's explanation about "some dumb kids" having caused the scratch.

12 African Roots

KV 12.1

Aufgabe 3 *Individuelle Lösungen, die ggf. folgende Aspekte umfassen:*

Both Barack Obama's and Nelson Mandela's biography could be said to exemplify that realizing *the American Dream* has become possible for colored people as well. Against all odds both managed to become president of their country, as the political situation changed towards more equality of members of all ethnic backgrounds. However, this only seems to be a development of very recent years as the destiny of previous civil right activists like Dr. Martin Luther King – an educated man and brilliant orator himself – shows: he was assassinated for his political involvement.

KV 12.2

1. **African Roots:** Atlantic triangular slave trade.
   Alex Haley's story of Kunta Kinte
2. **Slavery:** Black slaves in America / the Caribbean.
   Solomon Northup
3. **Segregation:** free, but not equal
4. **Apartheid in South Africa:**
   Nelson Mandela – civil rights activist, prisoner, President
5. **The Civil Rights Movement:**
   Dr. Martin Luther King
6. **The first Black American President of the United States:**
   Barack Obama

Inhalt Audio-CD:

Track 01: Will you be my Valentine? (6:46 min)
Track 02: Forgiving Katrina (6:33 min)
Track 03: Opa Joe (6:42 min)
Track 04: ABC (6:46 min)
Track 05: Escape to the USA (5:53 min)
Track 06: Divided Country (5:44 min)
Track 07: Freedom (6:47 min)
Track 08: Patriot (6:46 min)
Track 09: Indian Elvis (6:57 min)
Track 10: 13th Street (5:36 min)
Track 11: Servant of God (5:18 min)
Track 12: African Roots (6:18 min)

Abkürzungen:

KV   Kopiervorlage
SuS   Schülerinnen und Schüler
sb   *somebody*
sth   *something*

Symbole:

◎   Audio-CD
🙎🙎🙎   Gruppenarbeit
✍   Hausaufgabe
👂   Hörverstehensaufgabe
(www.)→ Internetrecherche
👄   mündliche Aufgabe
🙎🙎   Partnerarbeit
✎   schriftliche Aufgabe

Online-Link:

Alle in diesem Titel verwendeten Internetlinks finden Sie gesammelt in einem Word-Dokument.
Geben Sie den Code **6bt7aa** in das Suchfeld auf **www.klett.de** ein. Sie gelangen dann zu einer Internetseite mit der Linkliste zu diesem Titel.